Blessed to Survive:
The Thanksgiving Day Massacre

Patrick Knight

Campbell Wells Press

●　　●　　●　　●　　●

BLESSED TO SURVIVE
a novel by Patrick Knight

First Edition, July 2012

Copyright © 2012 by Patrick Knight

Author Services by Pedernales Publishing LLC
www.pedernalespublishing.com

Campbell Wells Press
5436 S. W. 191 Terrace
Miramar, Florida 33029

Author's Note: This is a true story of survival.
I have attempted to recreate events based on my
memory of them, information from the criminal
proceedings against the killer and/or witness
statements to the police and media outlets.

Library of Congress Control Number: 2012910155

ISBN: 978-0-9856905-0-2

Thanks to ...

St. Mary's ICU: Dr. Misquith, Dr. Hristov, Dr. West, Dr. Vega, Dr. Scharf, Dr. Osiyemi, Mounir, Rich, Antonio, Paul, Tom, Frank, Stephanie, Amber, Lou Ann, Sheryl, Danielle, Pamela, Kirsten, Julia, Michelle, Ethna, Wendy, Denise, Darlene, Sherrie, Antoinette, Megan, Connie, and so many others.

Mt. Sinai Rehab: Adam, Alex, Kate, Pam, Chris, Sue, Elizabeth, Hoang, Maria, Dr. Schram, and the entire staff.

Police and prosecutors: Jupiter Police Chief Frank Kitzerow, Detective Eric Frank, Aleathea McRoberts, Terri Skyles, Michael McAuliffe, and John Walsh from *America's Most Wanted.*

My parents, my brothers and their families, my friends, my coworkers, Dr. Alejandro del Valle, Alfredo Bless, Cathy, and especially my new wife, Jennifer.

Contents

Prologue

I had a blessed life prior to Thanksgiving Day, 2009. On that day, my late wife's brother shot my wife and other family members, leaving four dead.

He also shot me, and I entered a coma for three months. After I woke up, I had to relearn how to do everything, like a baby. I had never experienced any tragedy before, so I was ill-equipped to deal with it, but I've learned to move forward and find a perfect life in my new reality.

This is my story.

Blessed to Survive:

The Thanksgiving Day Massacre

Chapter One:

Waking Up from Deep Sleep

My eyelids fluttered. I looked up. As I fought to focus on my surroundings, I had no idea where I was, so I just lay in bed, blinked my eyes, and stared up at the ceiling. I tried to move my head to take in the room, but I could move it barely an inch either way. I could see the blue walls out of the corner of my eye. Then I remembered that I had been shot. I had never been a patient in the hospital before. It seemed strange. My mind started whizzing back and forth, trying to make sense of what I was seeing and feeling, trying to analyze all possibilities. I knew I had been shot in the stomach. I remembered that, for sure, because I remembered being curled up in the fetal position when the paramedics had arrived at the house. I also remembered that the paramedics had brought me by helicopter to the hospital.

It was weird, though, because I knew I had just been shot the night before, and yet I didn't feel the searing pain in my belly anymore. Could the wound have healed that fast? In just one day? Boy, these doctors were talented!

I could hear a bunch of machines that were beeping, whirring, and making other noises behind me. If I looked to the left, I could see machines stacked on top of other machines with bright lights that blinked or lines that moved up and down with my breathing. As I looked up at the ceiling again, I could see the television was on, but I couldn't focus on the picture.

I was too busy analyzing my situation.

Next I tried to open my mouth, but the lips felt stuck together. I moved them from left to right and back again and succeeded in peeling them apart. *Why are they so sticky?* I asked myself. I smacked my lips together a few times. There was something in my mouth! It felt like a tube. As I concentrated on it, I could feel it in the back of my mouth and down my throat. Being curious about this tube, I decided to reach up and touch it and find out how big it was and where it was attached. I tried to move my right arm. It wouldn't move. I tried the left arm. It wouldn't move, either.

What's going on here? I tried to lift my head, but that wasn't happening. *I can't believe this! I must be paralyzed. Are you kidding me?* I was starting to freak out, but I forced myself to remain calm. I mean, what was I going to do? Get up and scream? I couldn't move a muscle.

Thankfully, logic started to take over from fear, and I decided to see if maybe I could move my fingers and toes. I couldn't be paralyzed if I could move my fingers and toes. Starting with my fingers, I tried to scratch the bed. *It's working! Thank you, thank you, thank you.* I could feel my fingers moving back and forth across the sheet. The rest of my hand did not seem to be moving, but at least the fingers were.

I tried my toes next. *Yes, yes, yes!* I could feel them wiggling under the sheet. One of my feet was moving slightly at the ankle. What a relief! There was movement in my fingers and toes. It still didn't explain why I couldn't move my arms or my legs, but at least I didn't feel totally paralyzed.

As I peered out of the corner of my eye toward the right, I saw two nurses enter the room. One of them walked up to the bed and leaned over and looked down on me. She was inspecting me closely. Then she leaned further in to look right into my eyes.

"Oh, you're awake," she said in a cheery voice. "He's awake," she shouted to some other people outside my room. Focusing her attention back on me, she asked, "How do you feel?"

I opened my mouth to answer her, but no sound came out. I smacked my lips and tried again, but still, there was no sound.

"Steven," she said, "you can't talk yet because you have a trach tube in your throat. But don't worry, you'll talk again. Do you feel okay?"

My first thought was *Who is Steven? My name is Patrick.* But she seemed nice and she had such a kind face, so I nodded as well as I could to let her know I felt fine.

"Do you know what the date is?" she asked.

I wasn't sure exactly, but I was sure that I'd been shot just the night before. Since she was asking me this question, though, maybe a few days had passed while I recovered from surgery. *Who knows?* I shook my head.

3

"It is February 24, 2010," she said.

Is this lady crazy? I was just shot on Thanksgiving Day, 2009. She can't possibly mean it's really February 24, 2010. I scrunched up my face and shook my head in an effort to show her I didn't believe her.

"Yes," she said. "Yes, it is, Steven. Here, look at my watch."

I looked. It said 24, but that didn't mean anything. *And why was she calling me Steven?*

"Look at the TV, Steven. See the date in the bottom corner of the screen?"

I can't remember which of the twenty-four hour news stations was on, but, sure enough, it said February 24, 2010. Now my mind went into overdrive as I tried to comprehend this sudden lapse of time. I had been asleep for three months? That didn't seem possible. I was in complete disbelief, and now my brain was racing, trying to make sense of this news. *Three months?*

But it was indeed true. I had come into the hospital on the night of Thursday, November 26, 2009, Thanksgiving night, with a serious gunshot wound to the stomach. As I learned a bit later, because the killer got away after the killing and was still on the loose, the hospital had given me the alias, Steven, when they admitted me.

My injury was severe, as there was a hole in my stomach and the bullet had also pierced a kidney. Nobody had thought I would make it. The doctors and nurses at St. Mary's Hospital in West Palm Beach, Florida, had worked overtime to save me as everyone else prayed for a miracle.

I had been asleep for three months because they had induced a coma so they could deal with the myriad of complications I endured during that time. For starters, I had infections throughout my body. Apparently, this had something to do with my being shot in the stomach right after eating a large Thanksgiving dinner. The food had spilled out of my stomach and found its way into the various nooks and crannies of my body, where it caused some pretty serious infections.

The doctors had to go inside me at least three times to search for the locations of certain infections. Sometimes they had looked but remained stumped as to the source of the problem. In other words, there were times they were having difficulty even finding the infection. I know these infections must have been pretty serious because I was told that the doctors had not hesitated to keep opening me up for more surgery. Trust me, I still have the massive scars to prove it.

As for my family, all these infections had presented them with a roller-coaster ride of emotions. There was an infection. The doctors got it. Another infection popped up. The doctors told my parents to prepare for the worst. Maybe I wasn't going to make it this time. But each infection eventually subsided and I came through…until another one crept in somewhere else in my body. Another round of surgery ensued. This cycle of serious and minor infections continued on a weekly basis throughout the three months of my coma.

I also learned that my brother was sending out text messages to my closest friends and other family members to update them with my condition. Each weekly report gave them hope or gave them chills. One week, the message would be that a particular surgery was successful. The next week, it would seem like I was not going to make it to Saturday. Everyone who had been reading these texts has told me that at one point or another, they had nearly given up hope. Three months is just too long to be in a coma and wake up.

To make matters worse, I contracted pneumonia at one point and had a severe fungus in my lungs. Even after I woke up, every time I coughed, this nasty green mucous flew out of my mouth. My kidneys also presented a huge problem during the coma: one of them had been removed, and the other one quit working for a month. Thank goodness, I was sleeping during the dialysis I received every other day. My parents told me that the nurse working that machine kept going crazy because the numbers on the machine would shoot up and then down with no explanation, making various alarms go off.

The complications were compounded one after another. There was still that hole in my stomach, which made feeding me a very difficult task. My white blood cell count was more than double the normal count. Due to all the fluids pumped inside me, my body had swollen to nearly 275 pounds. My head ballooned to the size of a pumpkin. My arms were incredibly swollen, and my hands were the size of baseball gloves. My legs were saturated with fluids.

And my heart went out of rhythm for an extended period of time. I was told that I only survived because I had been in such good aerobic shape prior to the shooting. My blood pressure was also extremely high, reaching near stroke levels at times, and I also had pancreatitis, which is an inflammation of the pancreas and is considered a life-threatening condition.

I am not sure how I survived.

In fact, during one of the more dire moments, a doctor pulled my parents aside and told them that I had less than one percent chance of surviving. He also told them that even if I survived, I might be a vegetable or, at the very least, I would have severe brain damage and memory loss. One of the first nurses who saw me after I woke up told me that I had been "deader than dead" in the operating room. But the doctors never gave up. They kept pulling me back from the brink of extinction. On one occasion, I nearly died coming out of the CAT scan room when I wasn't getting enough oxygen. I was turning blue. This of course happened just as they were rolling my gurney past where my parents were sitting. They got a full view. Imagine the feelings of despair they had as their youngest child went past them turning blue and the nurses were calling for emergency actions because they were losing me.

Everything that happened to my body during those three months pointed to the worst possible outcome. I was surely going to die, and if I didn't die, my future life would not be a life worth living. About one week before I woke up, another terrible infection had permeated my body and the doctors hadn't been able to figure out how to stop it. The head nurse called my parents in and told them that I wouldn't make it past a few more days and they should begin making funeral arrangements. If seeing me turn blue hadn't discouraged them, imagine the feeling of utter despair they must have felt being told that their son was about to die.

Miraculously, however, my body found the infection by itself and figured out how to defeat it. My body wasn't ready to die. The one kidney I had left also decided to start working again after one month of hibernation.

Two days after being warned that I was dying, when my parents came back, the nurse approached them with a huge smile on her face. She told them the good news about the infection and added that my kidney was functioning again, too. The doctors had decided they could finally try to bring me out of the medically induced coma. What a change of fortune. What a miracle!

That first week after I woke up was a little hazy. I was fully conscious and awake, but I was also pretty groggy. I remember my parents standing over me, trying to gauge my mental status. This was frustrating for me because I could hardly talk and could barely move my head, which made it difficult to communicate. I couldn't tell anyone about all the things that were going through my mind in those first several days.

My parents tried to find out what I remembered from the incident and before. I mouthed to them that I knew I had been shot and that I remembered everything. I told them who shot me and responded affirmatively with a nod when they asked me if I remembered being in the helicopter and in the emergency room.

That was true. I remembered every detail of the incident from the minute my eyes opened. But there was one thing I didn't know because I hadn't seen it happen. I had no idea what had happened to my wife.

It is interesting see the human brain works to examine and justify various situations. During that first week of consciousness, I didn't see my wife Lisa, not even one time. My parents came a lot, and sometimes Lisa's parents were there. My brother and his wife came to visit me. But no Lisa.

Lying there, I just figured that Lisa was so pregnant that they weren't allowing her to come into the ICU. I also assumed that whoever wasn't visiting me on a particular day must be spending time with Lisa. After all, she would be nearly five months pregnant by now, so I was sure that she was struggling without me there to assist her. I felt bad that I hadn't been able to be there for these past three months, but it never dawned on me to ask anyone if she had been shot, too. My mind had already concocted the exact reason for her absence from the ICU.

Since I was in a Catholic hospital, priests came in on a regular basis to visit me. One day toward the end of that first week, a priest came into my room to see how I was doing and to pray for me. Apparently, my parents had asked him to break some terrible news to me.

I had no idea how bad this news would end up being. He told me a bunch of things about placing my hope in God and about how I was a miracle for surviving this tragedy. He was very nice, and his words comforted me a bit until he asked me, innocently enough, if he could pray with me and I nodded. About five or six sentences into the prayer, he said the following chilling words: "And, Lord, please let her watch over him from heaven. Please let her be his guardian angel."

My eyes popped open. I looked at my mother. I still couldn't talk, so I mouthed the words, "Who? Who? Lisa?"

The second I saw my mother's eyes welling up with tears, I knew the answer. My heart sank. My head started spinning. *Lisa is dead?* How could I accept that? I was already dealing with my own tragedy, so how could I add the loss of my wife to this burden? I started to cry myself, and it wasn't just a little weeping, either. It was an uncontrollable flood of tears and trembling that started in my stomach and flowed through my whole body. My body convulsed and retched at the same time. My chest rose and fell as I struggled to even breathe. If I could have wailed aloud, I would have done so, but I couldn't make a sound. From that day forward, I faced the unenviable task of dealing with my own personal tragedy of a severe injury at the same time as I was grieving for the loss of my beautiful wife.

How could all of this be happening? My life had been so blessed before the incident. Everything was in place for Lisa and me to start our own family. I couldn't believe it. She couldn't be dead. I was not equipped to deal with more tragedy, nor was I ready to accept it. This was surreal!

My brain began searching for answers as I replayed every second of that horrific November night.

Chapter Two:

Thanksgiving Day, 2009.
Inside the Mind of a Killer

Thanksgiving day started off pretty much like every other Thanksgiving day during the past five years. My wife and I had made the two-hour drive from Miami up to Jupiter, Florida, to stay at the family condo with her parents. We went up there every year to visit my wife's extended family, which included her aunt and uncle, her cousin and her husband, and their six-year old daughter. My wife's other relatives from Miami also made the trip to Jupiter to join us, along with Lisa's twin sister, Carla.

This year, Lisa's cousins were hosting Thanksgiving dinner at their home, and everyone was to arrive at about 4 p.m. In total, there were sixteen people there to celebrate the holiday. I had been coming up to Jupiter with my wife for the last five years and the location would typically alternate between her uncle's house and her cousin's house. I knew what to expect, and this year seemed no different than any other.

Lisa's cousin made her special sweet potato soufflé, her aunt made the beans and rice, and her mom roasted the turkey. The food was always interesting because Lisa's family was Lebanese, though they came from Haiti. Every holiday meal thus had a little American-Caribbean-Middle Eastern twist. When you walked in the front door, you could smell the spices in the air. The turkey was a golden brown and juices ran down the sides when you cut into it. The rolls were so hot the butter melted on them as soon as it touched the bread. All throughout dinner, all you heard were laughter, stories, and more laughter. It was the kind of Thanksgiving they show in television commercials when they're trying to get you in the holiday spirit. It was pure joy.

After the main course, we all settled down to talk or watch a little football. We were too stuffed to have dessert yet, so different people gathered in the living room, dining room, or family room to carry on small conversations.

The way the house is set up, you enter the living room, which is connected to the dining room. If you exit the dining room to the right, you enter the kitchen and family room area. It's a big kitchen with a shelf bar for serving food that separates it from the family room on the other side. In order to get to the family room from the living room, you walk past the dining room, go through a doorway to the kitchen, walk all the way across the room to go around the shelf bar, and enter the family room through a narrow opening at the end of the bar. I had never given this layout much thought before, but it affected the events that occurred that night.

At some point, while we were having our small conversation, my wife's brother phoned my father-in-law and said that he was on his way to Jupiter. (Note that I refuse to use his name. I will refer to him only as the killer or as my wife's brother.) When I heard my father-in-law giving directions to the killer, I was surprised because he had never been at any family gatherings before. The family always got together in Jupiter three or four times a year. The killer had never been to a single gathering, not at Christmas, Thanksgiving, Easter, the Fourth of July, or Labor Day. He had never even met his little six-year-old cousin.

There was a reason that he had never come to any family gatherings. I learned a whole lot more about the killer and this family after the massacre, but at the time, I just knew that he was a bit estranged not only from the entire extended family but also from his own immediate family. According to the family, the killer was basically a failure at life in every aspect. His parents had him convinced that he would go to Harvard and be a high profile lawyer or doctor, but he had difficulty handling the rigors of undergraduate work at the University of Miami and was starting to realize that he was not cut out to be a success in the professional world.

Interestingly, he always blamed his inability to hack it in school—or later in the working world—on the fact that he'd had mononucleosis while in college. So here he was at the age of thirty-five without having succeeded in college, without having gone to law school or medical school, without ever having worked a day in his life, without ever having had a girlfriend. Basically, he was living like a hermit. His parents fully supported him. They had bought him a new car and rented beautiful condos for him in the ritzy parts of Miami, like Coral Gables and Brickell Avenue. They bought his food, paid his expenses, and gave him spending money. They also told him where to go and controlled his every action. That being said, he spent his days sitting in his condo watching television and playing on his computer. He rarely left his condo unless it was to get some food.

The killer was about five feet, seven inches tall and he had to weigh about 250 pounds. He had developed sleep apnea and had to use a breathing mask because he had difficulty breathing at night. He wore glasses that were too small for his round face, and in his early thirties he was already losing his hair. He was a negative and angry person. He was jealous of his two sisters, of me, and of anyone else who was doing something with their lives. The weirdest thing about him, though, was the hatred he expressed toward various groups of people. The killer was Lebanese. He hated Jews. He could not stop talking about them and how they were the cause of all evil in the world. If you have ever seen the movie *Borat*, then you have an idea what the killer was like, except this was real life, not a movie.

But it wasn't just Jews he hated. He had no respect for women. He felt that blacks were beneath him. I had only met him four or five times during the four years I knew Lisa and had always found it interesting that, considering how he turned out, this guy would have a negative opinion about anyone else. The group of people he was most vocal against, however, was homosexuals.

He constantly made jokes about them and talked bad about them. At first, I thought it was just another group that he hated, but I soon noticed that he was more vocal about them than the other people he hated. It was like he had something to prove.

I used to have regular conversations with my wife and her sister about the fact that we felt that the killer might be gay himself. We often gave each other sly glances when he went into one of his anti-gay tirades. The killer was effeminate, but that wasn't the only reason for our suspicions. If you spent just a couple hours with him, you got a sense that he might be confused about his sexual identity. His tirades merely confirmed that for us.

During the course of their investigation, the police discovered one witness who had come to the home of the killer's parents when he still lived there. The witness stated that the parents had not been there. The killer had opened the door wearing a dress. When the killer saw that the person at the door was apparently not who he was expecting, he slammed the door closed and wouldn't answer it again. The prosecutors asked me about this incident and the killer's cross-dressing, but I wasn't aware of these activities. It didn't surprise me, though, and it didn't bother me that he might be gay. I don't judge people. Certainly, being gay did not make him a bad person or a killer. But I think this dichotomy between his sexual desires and his Lebanese macho image was a major source of his anger.

When the killer's medical records were released to the media in 2011, they showed even stranger things in his past. He had a very dark side to him. Most of his thoughts were not based in reality. His psychiatric records show him being obsessed with death going back ten years before this incident. The doctors felt that he had unrealistic expectations of himself, which makes sense, given that he was an abject failure in life. Nobody told him he was a failure. He felt that he was entitled to be a powerful lawyer or a doctor without earning it. In fact, his father continued to speak highly of him despite his failure to accomplish anything. Another problem the killer had was that he was obsessed with germs. His medical records show that sometimes he saw germs on everything. He also saw blood everywhere. There were even times he skipped meals because he was afraid the food was contaminated.

Thanks to his inability to make something of his life, he also had a long history of depression. Doctors noted that he would often pace around the examination room and avoid direct eye contact. They also diagnosed him on multiple occasions with psychomotor retardation, and the records show that he continued sucking his thumb into his mid-twenties.

There is no doubt that for over a decade the killer had issues, and his ego only made things worse. He had tried to commit suicide twice. In 1999, he had shot himself in the chest and was rushed to the ER. Lisa had told me about that incident and the effect it had on the family. In 2005, he tried to kill himself again with an overdose of medications. He couldn't even succeed in suicide. His obsession with death did not, however, end with his thinking about taking his own life. After his two suicide attempts, the medical records show that he had vowed to kill himself and take his family with him. On multiple occasions, he threatened to kill his family. He swore that he was going to slit his sister Carla's throat.

His father had told the doctors that he was so concerned about his son having a gun that he (the killer's father) had gone to all the local gun shops in Miami in 2000 and begged them not to sell any more guns to his son. He was afraid of what his son might do if he were able to get his hands on another gun. A little more than nine years later, the killer showed exactly what he would do with guns.

The killer's records also show that when he was hospitalized, he became agitated, aggressive, and combative toward the doctors and nurses. He expressed worries about "burning eternally in hell" for trying to kill himself in the suicide attempts. Because of his fears, he avoided using the words "God," "Jesus," and "Virgin Mary."

The medical records also show that in 2006 he threatened to kill his family on a continual and constant basis. He believed his entire family was plotting against him. He hated his family and was jealous of his sisters. He wanted them dead. He was miserable because he had turned out to be such a failure while his sisters were living such productive and happy lives.

There were even several episodes during the ten years before the shooting when the killer was hospitalized and received electroconvulsive therapy. This is commonly known as shock treatment. I didn't even know they still did that kind of therapy, but the records show that he sometimes got it four times in one hospitalization. During one visit, after receiving the shock therapy, he began to tie his shoelaces over and over again and was not able to respond to the nurse's directions to stop.

According to Lisa, the real problem was that you never knew which of her brother's symptoms were real and which ones were made up. Over the course of his treatments in the ten years prior to the shooting, he came up with many different kinds of symptoms and "diseases" that he claimed to have. There is ample evidence of these claims in his medical records. He got on his computer and researched various diseases that there is no way to objectively prove or disprove, then he started to exhibit symptoms of the disease and claim that it kept him from working or being productive in society.

I remember one conversation with the killer when he went on for fifteen minutes, telling me about the research he had done regarding chronic fatigue syndrome. He had researched both causes and symptoms, he said, and he told me about all the different medications used to treat the ailment. He knew various theories about the syndrome and told me who the top specialists were in that field. He had easily spent sixty hours doing this research over the course of a week. In the end, he said that he felt that he had chronic fatigue syndrome. That explained why he was unable to work. His researching skills were impressive, and so I suggested that he become a paralegal and try to work at a medical malpractice law firm. I told him that law firms need people like him who can do such exhaustive research on medical conditions and their causes.

But his only reaction to my suggestion was to be stunned as he realized that his story had backfired. Rather than making me feel sorry for him, sorry that he had this new medical condition, his story had proved to me that he could work and that he was very savvy on a computer.

I will never forget his response. He looked at me with a straight face and told me that he couldn't work because he wouldn't be able to read a computer screen long enough. He told me that he would likely get headaches if he had to do that kind of work. In truth, he would never be a mere paralegal; he was supposed to have been a Harvard lawyer.

I didn't push it, but our conversation showed me how far he was willing to go to convince people that it wasn't his fault he had no job. Clearly, he was able to sit on his computer for five or ten hours at a time. That's all he ever really did in his condo. He was either researching medical issues or reading blogs to gather more information for his hate-filled tirades.

Once the killer committed to this story about mononucleosis causing his downward spiral, he had to either fully commit to it for life or admit that he was a failure. But he was never going to admit to failure. He couldn't tolerate the thought of admitting to being a failure at life, so he just withdrew from life. He stayed in his condo most days and kept a low profile during the four years I was involved with this family. The family never let me know the extent of his hate and denial. When Lisa shared a few things with me, like his first suicide attempt, her parents got mad at her. They had hoped to use this Thanksgiving dinner in 2009 to reintroduce their son into the family because they felt he was doing better. But he wasn't invited because he still harbored bitter feelings toward his sisters, his uncle, and other family members.

For that reason, everyone but his parents was surprised to hear that the killer was on his way.

As I learned later, during the week leading up to Thanksgiving, the killer had started asking very detailed questions of his parents concerning where dinner would be held, what time it would start, and who would be in attendance. When he came to his parents' house and asked for his passport, they gave to him. He had also bought a car cover for his car and shredded all the documents in his house. When his parents asked him why he was shredding everything, he told them that he just wanted a fresh start. He also told his parents that he was no longer taking his medications.

And in spite of all these red flags, his parents hoped he was getting better and told him that he could come up for Thanksgiving dinner. They did not, however, tell anyone he was coming because the prior year, when his sister Carla had asked her uncle if the killer could come to the dinner, the uncle had said no.

I also learned later that in the days before Thanksgiving, Lisa's mother had hosted an open house. This was not uncommon, as Lisa and her mom were realtors who worked together as partners. The killer had stopped by this open house and asked more questions about Thanksgiving. This time, he asked his mother what time they thought the dinner would be ending. His questions were specific and pressing.

At some point, Lisa also arrived at the open house. During her conversation with her brother, she told him that she was pregnant. With zero emotion and no response, he turned away and walked out of the house. Their mother looked at Lisa and said, "I hope he doesn't come to kill us all."

But I knew nothing about any of these things before the shooting. I didn't know he was a sociopath. I certainly didn't suspect that the killer was spending so much time plotting the massacre of his family, the Thanksgiving massacre that would change our lives forever.

Chapter Three:

The Massacre

When the killer arrived at his cousin's house on Thanksgiving night, he was acting perfectly normal. He was introduced to his six-year old cousin for the first time, and then he greeted everyone else. At that time, we had just put out the desserts. The killer picked up a couple pieces of pie and cake and sat down at the table with me, his two sisters, and a few other people.

We had very normal conversation about football, some of my legal cases, and some interesting things in the news. There were no warning signs to signal what was going to happen later that evening. I have often thought about his actions before he shot us all. You would think that someone about to commit mass murder would be shifty or act nervous. Maybe they would be sweating profusely, or maybe they would be looking around incessantly. But the killer was so calm and normal; we were completely caught off-guard.

He finished his pie and took a drink from his water glass. I guess this was his final nourishment before his big moment.

After dessert, we all went into the living room for what I always called The Talent Show. It seemed like everyone in this family had some kind of talent, from singing to playing piano. It was a real Hallmark moment kind of thing. Lisa and Carla always sang one or two duets because everyone loved to hear the twins sing. Other relatives sometimes sang as well. That night, someone sang in French. Lisa's fifteen-year-old cousin usually played the piano, but that night he did a series of impressions that were spot-on. They always tried to get me to do something like juggle or show off some other stupid talent I had, but on that night I convinced them to let me just tell a Thanksgiving Day joke. Here is the last joke I told before I was shot:

> A missionary was walking through the jungle, looking for a village where he could spread the Good Word. All of a sudden, a lion jumped out of the bushes in front of him and let out a huge roar. The missionary closed his eyes, fell to his knees, and shouted, "Dear God, please turn this lion into a Christian!" There was a loud boom, a flash of light, and a cloud of smoke. When the smoke cleared, the missionary saw the most amazing sight. There was the lion down on his knees, head bowed, eyes closed, and paws folded. The missionary smiled and sighed. Then the lion prayed, "Dear God, thank you so much for this food that I am about to eat."

The final act of the evening was always performed by Lisa's six-year-old cousin, who had multiple talents. She could play the piano, recite Bible verses, sing songs, and dance. She loved to dance and was not shy about doing a whole ballet recital for the family. Because she was only six, it was an amazing show.

Since the living room was not big, I ended up sitting in a chair next to the killer. We were the only two in the back of the room. I turned to him and said, "Isn't she cute?" "Adorable," he replied. Who could imagine that he was only twenty minutes away from his own act, one of unthinkable horror?

The show over, the family returned to the kitchen and family room for coffee. Conversations were wrapping up after about fifteen or twenty minutes, and I asked Lisa if we could leave. In this family, there were always long good-byes. You had to go around to each person individually and say one last thing and then give them a kiss on the cheek. It would often take half an hour or more to get out of the house, so you couldn't wait until you were super exhausted before you started the process.

When I mentioned leaving to Carla, she decided to come with us. We wrapped up some food to take with us and started to walk through the kitchen. Carla and I were the first people into the kitchen while Lisa was still saying her good-byes...her last good-byes.

As we started to walk through the kitchen, we saw the killer standing there by himself. I told him we were leaving. As I shook his hand, he said, "Why don't you stay a little longer?" I smiled, shook my head, and told him we were tired and needed to go to bed. Then I turned toward my sister-in-law, Carla, to take the food she was carrying.

In the next minute, my life changed forever.

BANG. BANG. It sounded like a stick of dynamite was going off in my ear. My ears were ringing like a thousand old-style telephones going off at once. I was completely discombobulated. I felt like I had been punched in the stomach. I had been shot, but at that point I didn't realize it.

As I turned to look at the kitchen doorway, I saw the killer standing with a gun in his hand, raising it to point it at my head. Through all the commotion, I could see the barrel of the gun and the smoke still coming out of it. Instinctively, I threw the food at his face and flung myself to my left. The killer shot and missed.

Carla had dropped to one knee. I picked her up and dove out of the kitchen into the dining room. We landed with a thud, and I rolled off Carla and looked around to see what was happening. The killer took another step into the kitchen. *BANG. BANG. BANG.* I heard screams and people scrambling to get out of the way.

"He's got a gun!" I yelled from the floor. "Call 9-1-1. He's got a gun."

Obviously annoyed at my yelling, the killer turned and stood over my body and pointed the gun at my head. By this time, things were hazy, but I was in survival mode. There was a gun just four feet away from me and aimed at my head. I started moving my head back and forth so he wouldn't have an easy target. *BANG*. A bullet ripped through my shirt collar, barely grazing my right shoulder. *BANG*. A bullet hit the floor just past the left side of my head.

Later, when I woke up in the hospital, I realized just how close the killer had come to putting a bullet in my head. The police officers had the shirt I was wearing in evidence and told me that there was a clear bullet hole in the collar just inches from my head. My shoulder also had a slight abrasion caused by the bullet making contact with my skin. I'm thankful that the killer was as incompetent with a gun as with everything else in his life. If he had known how to shoot a gun skillfully, I wouldn't be here to write this.

After trying to finish me off, the killer turned his attention back to the kitchen. I later learned from the police investigators about the horrors in the other room. The shooting continued, the killer firing from the kitchen into the family room where members of his family were like sitting ducks.

I was on the floor. My head was still ringing, and I was covering my ears. I tried to get up, but my body wouldn't cooperate. Between the shots, I could hear voices from the other room, but it seemed like the shots were coming in rapid succession. *BANG. BANG. BANG.*

I couldn't see what was happening in the next room, but I later learned a lot from the police investigative files and the statements of the other witnesses. The killer fired round after round at his family. They had nowhere to go. First, he shot Lisa, who was standing nearest to him. He shot her in the chest near her arm, and the bullet sliced right through her, puncturing her lungs.

He then turned his attention to the other members of the family. A few of them had escaped to the patio through the sliding glass doors, but most of them were still trapped in the family room. Some crouched down behind the couches or chairs, others dropped to the floor. Fear gripped us all.

At one point, the killer walked up to his seventy-three-year-old aunt and shot her in the chest. Everyone was begging him to stop and put the gun down, but immediately after he shot his aunt, her husband, who is a former doctor, tried to resuscitate her. The killer walked over to them and shot her again at point-blank range. She died instantly. Then he held the gun at his uncle's head. He despised his uncle. With everyone begging the killer to spare his uncle's life, he pulled the trigger. Nothing happened. Apparently, when he shot his aunt the second time, he held the gun too close to her chest and the gun powder went back up inside the gun, causing it to jam. He pulled the trigger again. Still nothing. Spooked by the gun's failure to fire, the killer turned and ran out of the kitchen.

In the meantime, I had dragged myself across the floor from the dining room into the living room, leaving a trail of blood behind me as my arms pulled my nearly lifeless body inch by inch across the floor. I reached for my cell phone and tried to dial 9-1-1, but the numbers on my BlackBerry were too small and I was shaking too much. I had heard the shooting stop, I saw the killer come running out of the kitchen and leap over Carla's body. He was so pudgy, it was an awkward jump, but he managed it. Then he came toward me. I tried not to move a muscle so he'd think I was dead and wouldn't shoot me again. But as he came down the hall, he didn't even look down at me. I kept my eyes open so I could see what he was going to do next. I turned my head and watched him run into one more room.

No, no, NO! I cried to myself. *Not the little girl's room.* BANG. I cringed. He shot her. As I stared down the hallway, I saw him come out as though he was going to leave the house. He paused for a second, then went back into the little girl's room. *BANG. BANG.* He was making sure she was dead.

I couldn't believe this was happening.

And then, as quickly as it started, it ended. I saw the killer run out the front door, and now all I could hear were the screaming and wailing coming from the kitchen and family room. I've never heard such grief-stricken crying. I could also hear people running around outside.

Eventually, all the noise stopped. I listened to hear who was still in the house, but I couldn't hear a single person. We had been left to die. I looked over at my sister-in-law. Her body was not moving. She had stopped moaning. The screaming outside seemed very distant. The shooting was over, the killer was gone, and now it was just me and death facing each other.

Chapter Four:

Facing Death

I was lying on the rug in the living room, and now as the intense ringing in my ears started to dissipate, my head started to clear up. Everything still seemed like it was happening in slow motion and in third person. I felt like I had been watching all this action rather than having been a part of it. I looked over at Carla's lifeless body about twenty feet away from me.

She's dead, I said to myself. *What is happening here?*

With those words, my mind began to think further. *I know the little girl must be dead, too, because he went back into her room a second time to make sure he finished the job. Others must have been shot, too. It's so quiet in this house now.*

I couldn't hear any more screaming or wailing. *Is everybody gone? Is everybody dead?*

I found out later that everyone who was still alive was outside the house. Inside, it was now a tomb inhabited by me and those who had been murdered. I'm not sure what was worse, the sounds of a gun being fired over and over, the screams and wailing that followed the shots, or this eerie silence. The silence felt thick and heavy.

What had happened weighed on my mind and my soul. I was in an awful place where I can very easily mentally transport myself to again because what happened there was something that I have never experienced before and hope to never experience again. Silence can produce a moment of clarity, but it also can lead to a moment of panic. My mind raced back and forth. How could I make sense of what I had just experienced?

My thoughts were soon interrupted by the searing pain in my stomach. Until then, I hadn't noticed where I had been shot. But now I certainly knew. I had felt the initial impact in my stomach in the kitchen, but I hadn't realized that a bullet had penetrated my body. Now it felt like someone was taking a nine-inch knife and stabbing me in the stomach again and again. The pain was so intense that I couldn't focus on anything else.

I was wearing a yellow shirt that day. I looked down and could see the huge blood stain over the left side of my stomach. It was getting bigger, second by second. It had started out the size of a quarter and quickly grown to be larger than an orange. Now the blood was coming out so fast my shirt couldn't absorb any more. My shirt started to act like a strainer, with the blood seeping out through the threads. It was as if a faucet of blood had been turned on.

Interestingly, I had no reaction to the sight of my blood. I couldn't react because the pain was ripping through me so hugely that instinct took over. I kept squirming around, trying to find a comfortable position. I rolled from my left side to my right side, but that didn't help. I tried straightening my body, but that made it worse. I finally found a somewhat tolerable position in a full fetal position lying on my left side, which is the side where I had been shot. I was wrapped into such a tight ball that I couldn't think of anything but the pain. Once I was able to regroup from the searing pain, however, my focus shifted to a whole new idea. I had only one thought.

I'm going to die.

There was no one there to help me. I was alone in the house. I couldn't believe that no one was coming back to help me or the others. They'd just left us there to die. I was sure that this was it. My life was ending.

People often ask me now if my whole life flashed before me or if I had any wild thoughts or memories. I guess they want to know what it's like to be on your deathbed knowing you are probably going to die.

Well, I'm just a little too pragmatic for all that philosophy. I knew exactly what I was doing, and I immediately started making sure God knew it, too. I didn't pray for survival. I prayed that I would go to heaven.

"Dear God," I managed to say, "I have been a Christian my whole life, and I know that I have been a sinner, but I have never lost my faith. I want to be in heaven with you. I believe that you are the One True God, and I believe that Jesus died on the cross to save me from my sins. Please bring me to heaven with you."

I think I prayed some version of that prayer out loud about five or six times while I was lying there on the rug. Looking back, I find it interesting that I didn't pray for survival. I had really started to lose hope. I have no idea how much time passed before the police and emergency rescue personnel arrived, but it seemed like an eternity.

The blood was pouring out of my stomach. I knew that if help didn't arrive soon, I would breathe my last breath. I was okay with that, but I just really wanted to make sure that if I did die on that day, I would be in heaven.

My prayers were finally interrupted by deep male voices and thundering footsteps.

"Fatal," I heard from one room.

"Fatal," I heard from where Carla was lying.

"Fatal," I heard from the kitchen.

"I've got one that's alive!" another voice shouted. I looked up and saw an officer standing over me. "Stay strong, buddy," he told me. "Hang on because paramedics are on their way."

And that's when I started to think I might survive. Amazingly, I still had all my faculties. I had not passed out, though every second was a major struggle to remain conscious. I couldn't tolerate the searing pain in my stomach. At least three times, I asked the officer how much longer it would be, and he just kept reassuring me that they were on their way. He asked me what happened, and I remember telling him that it was my wife's brother. "He shot everybody and ran out the front door," I said.

Finally, I could hear the officers directing the paramedics to me. The first thing they told me to do was let go of my cell phone, which I was holding in my right hand. I can laugh about it now, but I specifically remember what I was thinking at the time. Ten days earlier, Lisa and I bought our first smart phones. We had each purchased a BlackBerry, and I had been amazed at the difference between the new smart phones and our old cell phones. There was no way that I was going to lose my brand-new, awesome phone. They told me to let it go two or three times, and then someone just pried it out of my hand. I didn't put up much of a fight because what I wanted more than anything in the world was for them to make the pain go away. Once I let go of the phone, I tried to look down.

I wanted to see what the paramedics were doing to me. As I watched, they took out a scissors and started to cut my pants and my shirt off me. My hope of survival was gaining momentum with each action these paramedics took. As I regained my composure, I had a new prayer for God—

Dear God, please let me live. Give me strength to survive this incident. Guide their hands to make me better. I want to live. Please let me live. I don't want to die. And, please, please, please make this pain stop.

Once my shirt came off, I could see the big hole in my stomach with blood gushing out of it. That sight was not easy to process. I'd never seen my stomach look like that before. There was a big gash there, and my blood was everywhere. They tried to stop the bleeding, but the blood was just pouring out because my insides had been torn up.

The killer had used hollow-tip bullets. The hollow

tip bullet increases in size once it enters the body. It disrupts and damages more tissue. This maximizes tissue damage, blood loss, and shock. It's pure evil.

The paramedics continued to bandage me and check my mental faculties. Then came the questions.

"Sir, what is your name?"

"Patrick. Patrick Knight."

"What do you do for a living, Patrick?"

"I'm a lawyer."

"Where is your office?"

"Down in Miami."

"Where did you go to high school?"

"Timothy Christian High School."

Geez, I thought, *what's with all these dumb questions? We can make small talk later, AFTER you resolve this hole-in-my-stomach issue.* In reality, they were just trying to keep me awake and alert because I would have a better chance of survival.

After applying the bandages, and still asking questions to keep me alert, they put me on a gurney and rolled me out of the house. On the way down the driveway to the ambulance, I saw some of the other family members who had been inside. They were now standing on the lawn. Someone asked who was on the gurney, and I heard someone else respond that they thought it was Patrick. I continue to be amazed at the little details I can remember even though the pain in my stomach was overwhelming.

Inside the ambulance, the paramedics kept asking questions. They were really nice, but I tried a new direct approach now. I wanted to get knocked out.

"Did you ever have a dog?"

"Yes."

"What was his name?"

"Magic. Can you just knock me out?"

"Where were you born?"

"In Chicago. Seriously, guys, I know you're eventually going to knock me out. Can't you just do it now?"

"Not yet. Are you a Gator fan?"

"No. Yuck. Miami Hurricanes."

It kept on like this until we arrived at the helicopter.

Now that was an interesting experience. You have to remember that they had cut off all of my clothes, and even though they wrapped me in blankets, I could feel the draft on my exposed parts. The helicopter ride seemed quick and effortless. It was not exactly the way I had envisioned by first helicopter ride, but at least we arrived safely at St. Mary's Hospital in West Palm Beach. As they wheeled me into the emergency room, there were a few more questions, including did I have any allergies. After that, I finally got what I'd been asking for. I saw the nurse come up to me and ask me to just keep breathing normally while she administered a drug. It was as if someone pulled down the window shades over my eyeballs. I went into a deep sleep.

Meanwhile, the police raced over to my brother Brian's house in Miramar, Florida, which is about an hour south of Jupiter. As I learned later, they pounded on his door and asked for him to open up immediately. At this point, the police didn't know the killer's intent. They wanted to protect the family members of those who had been shot. They told Brian what had happened and then left a police squad car outside his door for protection.

Distraught and overwhelmed, Brian had the unenviable task of calling our mother and father, who were in Arizona. As he dialed his phone, he quickly devised a plan to tell them little by little. When our mother answered the phone, he told her to sit down. Then he said that there had been an incident and that I had been taken to the hospital. He described the shooting and said I was in critical condition.

As Mom became upset, he had to tell her there was more. He told her that Lisa had been murdered, that Carla had been murdered, that there were other victims. My parents were beside themselves with grief, but they immediately packed their bags and headed to South Florida for a five month journey of grieving, praying, and enduring feelings of hopelessness.

As for me, I had just begun day one of a three-month deep sleep. The last thing I remember is the nurse leaning over me and telling me to breathe normally. I took a few breaths and started to feel calm. I could feel things fading to black, and then I was out.

My next memory is of February 24, 2010.

Chapter Five:

My First Days Awake

Every one of those first few days I was awake in the ICU was certainly a new experience. The medications often made me groggy and I sometimes fell asleep in the middle of a conversation. When I was awake, my mind was usually racing and searching for answers. What had really happened? Why it had been allowed to happen? Then my thoughts would shift to my present situation as I tried to take in everything that was happening now. Lying there, I couldn't even think about the future because I was still trying to grapple with the present. This is a lesson that I learned very quickly in the ICU: Don't panic or worry about the future until you know all the facts about the present.

Day by day, I listened to the nurses talking to me or my parents about my condition. I couldn't move my arms an inch in any direction and my neck was so weak I could only give a feeble nod or shake in answer to questions. I think I was actually "speaking" with my eyes. The nurses always seemed to know what I was thinking when I looked at them. What I wanted them to know was that I was paying attention, that I wanted to cooperate and get to a quick recovery. Quick recovery? Yeah, right. Little did I know just how bad my condition was.

I watched the nurses closely. Each one had a different style, but they always gave me a play-by-play commentary to explain what they were doing and why they were doing it. This helped me a lot because I felt very fragile and weak and extremely dependent. I mean, I couldn't move or talk. My frustration level was building day by day.

"Okay, Steven," one of the nurses would tell me, "we're going to move you onto your left side so we can change the sheets. We're going to lift the sheet and roll you onto your side. But don't worry, we'll make sure that you don't hit your head on the rail."

I didn't really have any choice. They did what they had to do, but I was grateful that they made me feel like I was involved in the process. When they changed the sheets, they counted to three and then lifted up quickly. I felt my body roll over. But it was very awkward. It always crashed against the side rail. *Wow, that's weird*, I always thought. *My body feels like a sack of potatoes.*

It is hard to explain what it feels like to have almost no muscles in your body. Nothing is pulling in your abdominal area to stabilize your body. Your arms don't move upward instinctively to stop your momentum. Your face just falls into the pillow as it is slammed down because your neck muscles aren't strong enough for you to move into a more comfortable position. Getting the sheets changed under me was the first of many very humbling experiences I had in the hospital.

Every day, I continued to take stock of my situation. Between the nurses and my parents, I was learning a lot about what was going on. For instance, there was a tube in my mouth that was draining fluids from my stomach. I couldn't eat anything through my mouth because my stomach still had that hole in it, so they decided that the best way to feed me was to stick a tube up my nose and down my throat, bypassing my stomach and attaching to my intestines. I could thus "eat" a liquid meal filled with essential nutrients and vitamins without risking further problems in my stomach.

When they first explained the intubation procedure to me, I thought it sounded painful. I was sure I would be knocked out before they started. Wrong! For this procedure, they wheeled me up to the operating room and laid me on a cold metal table. Considering I had no muscle or fat on me at this point, my bones were poking into that metal table and I was almost unendurably uncomfortable. I had lost over fifty pounds at this point, and it was not a good feeling to have my tailbone, spine, ribs, shoulder blades, and elbows all flush against that cold, cold metal.

Have you ever pressed your elbows as hard as you can into a metal table? Have you ever hit your tailbone so hard you feel the pain all the way through the bone? Have you ever tried to move your feet when you're lying on a table because it feels like your heels are digging into the metal? Well, I had all of those sensations going on at the same time as I lay on that cold metal.

And there was no anesthesia because I had to be awake to keep swallowing the tube after it was shoved up my nose and down into my throat. It was painful and annoying, especially since my throat muscles had forgotten how to swallow. I just wanted it to end.

I kept trying to breathe and swallow normally, but I couldn't. The nurses had to step in and hold my head still because I was thrashing it from side to side. I was nearly at a breaking point, in fact, when the doctor announced that he had the tube in place. All I knew was that I never wanted to have to go through that procedure again.

As I returned to my room, my mother and father came to my bedside. They explained all the other tubes that were still in my body. There were tubes draining fluids from my chest and other tubes that were allowing my body to function properly. I had a big tracheotomy in my throat that allowed me to breathe the oxygen being supplied to me by a machine. There were other tubes coming out of me, and I never quite knew what they all were for.

To add to what I felt was a circus-like atmosphere, I still had five to ten different machines stacked up behind me and beside my bed, all of them beeping, whirring, and blinking. I learned real fast that I could make nurses come into my room by setting off one of the machines. If I coughed too much, one machine would sound its alarm. If I could get my pulse up by tapping my finger constantly, a different machine would sound its alarm. It's amazing how you learn to adapt in certain situations.

I was astonished when my parents said that all these tubes and machines were much fewer than what had been in me during the three months I was asleep. Again, I could only find solace in the fact that the worst stuff had happened while I was sleeping.

My mother suddenly remembered something and leaned over my bed. "You know why they call you Steven, right?"

Oh, yeah—they'd been calling me Steven again today. I was just getting used to it. I assumed they didn't know who I was or that they were just mistaken. I shook my head. Very gingerly.

My mom continued. "They call you Steven because that's your alias." I blinked in surprise, and she added, "When you're a victim of a violent crime and the killer is still on the loose, they give you a fake name so no one knows where you are. It also keeps the press away." She smiled. "Did you think they just didn't know your name?"

I tried returning her smile to let her know that was exactly what I'd been thinking. This made sense. *Wait a minute. The killer is still on the loose?*

"Where is [the killer]?" I asked, though no sound came from my mouth.

When she saw the distressed look on my face, her expression became instantly serious.

"He's in jail."

The killer had been on the run for over a month after the shooting. From what I heard from her and the TV newscasts, after he shot me and killed four people, he left the scene and drove south to the Florida Keys, where he went into hiding for about forty days. He registered at a motel using a fake name and paid cash for his stay, he hid his car under the car cover he had bought the week before, and then he just sat in his motel room day after day, hiding from the world. He did everything possible to stay inconspicuous, and the hotel owners had no idea there was a killer in one of their rooms.

There was a large coordinated effort to organize a manhunt. Police in three counties assisted the Jupiter police in searching for him. My friends also spent a day distributing flyers to local businesses from Fort Lauderdale down to Miami and posted the killer's picture in as many places as possible. In addition, Lisa's cousin, the father of the little girl who'd died, was constantly in the media, trying to keep the story alive and fresh in the minds of the public.

Ultimately, *America's Most Wanted* (*AMW*) became involved in the case. They did an elaborate online story on the shooting and the background of the killer, including videos, photos and identifying information to help people find him. The TV show, which was a condensed version of their online story and featured the famous $100,000 reward for the killer's capture, was set to air on a Sunday night right after the afternoon football games. As a preview to the show, *AMW* had several commercials airing during the football game. These commercials included clear pictures of the killer.

And it "just happened" that the owners of the motel where the killer was staying saw those commercials while they were watching the football game. They recognized the killer as the man staying in their motel. Then they started putting the pieces of the puzzle together. Their guest rarely left his motel room, he kept his car covered, he never wanted any maids changing the sheets in his room, and he only paid in cash. Now they became worried. Their own daughter was staying in the room right next to the killer. They immediately called her and told her to leave her room. At the same time, one of the owners tip-toed outside and looked under the car cover to see what kind of car the man hiding in the room had. Of course, even though it had a fake license plate, it matched the description in the commercial for the *AMW* episode. The motel owner called *AMW*'s hotline number and told the police that she was certain that the killer was staying in her motel. When the operator asked her how sure she was on a scale of one to 10, she didn't hesitate a second. "It's a 10." The U.S. marshals now got involved and immediately made their way down to the Keys.

A few hours later, as the killer was getting ready to watch himself on television, federal agents and other law enforcement officers burst into his room, crashing through the barricade the killer had put up to keep people out. After setting off a flash bomb, the officers apprehended him in his bathroom. They had to Taser him for noncompliance.

I later watched the entire take-down on the *AMW* website. At one point, the killer was begging for his life. Imagine that. The cowardly killer, a man who had shot a six-year-old girl, who kept shooting when his victims begged for their lives, was now begging for his own life.

Hearing this story in the hospital from my mother was so surreal. It sounded like an episode of *Law & Order*, not my life. Seriously, this stuff happens in TV shows and movies and weird news stories. But no one actually knows anyone that this stuff happens to, right? It is still surreal to me that my story remains on the website of *America's Most Wanted*, including the take-down video.

Plus, the people that died that day were four of the kindest people that ever lived on this planet. My late wife, Lisa, and her twin sister, Carla, were liked by everyone who met them. They weren't just kind, however, but perhaps a little naïve as well. This made them sweet. They enjoyed every new adventure in life. They were always smiling. They were selfless and were always trying to do things for other people.

This seems to be a common thread among the victims, because Lisa's aunt was also selfless in the way she acted on daily basis. It was almost as if she only cared for others and never did anything for herself. And then, of course, there was Lisa's six-year-old cousin, a child who loved God so much that she would actually do little theater shows about stories from the Bible. Why did these four people get taken from the earth?

In those first days I was awake, I often considered these questions, and more. Having nothing else to do, I was thinking all the time. Sometimes, I focused on my medical condition and what was happening in the hospital around me. Other times, I asked God why this had happened to me or to the other victims. Finally, there were those times that I just lay there thinking about what an amazing life I'd had before....

Chapter Six:

Unprepared for Tragedy

Prior to the shooting, I had never really experienced tragedy or loss. The closest thing to a loss occurred in 1999, when my mother had a heart attack and nearly died. Like me, she wasn't supposed to survive. But she did survive, and although the top two thirds of her heart still do not work, she has lived a very normal life for the past twelve years. She works out most days and does ballroom dancing nearly every night. My mom is truly amazing. She's a major inspiration to me in the way she bounced back and kept moving forward.

But that averted tragedy did not, alas, prepare me very well for one of the worst tragedies imaginable. The truth is that before I was shot, I felt that I had a very blessed life. By no means was I the richest and most successful guy in the world, but I felt truly blessed by the many accomplishments and successes I had experienced in my life. I grew up in Chicago and had a pretty normal Midwestern upbringing. My parents have now been married for over fifty years and were always very involved in the lives of their kids. I have two big brothers who were always there to play with me and teach me how to be better at sports. I went to nice private Christian schools that kept me pretty sheltered for most of my life. In fact, during my grade school years through eighth grade, I never even had more than six people in my class.

The teachers at my high school, Timothy Christian, really cared about the students and still know my name and face whenever I get back up there to visit. I played varsity soccer and tennis, wrote for the sports section of the school newspaper, and did just about every other extra-curricular activity the school offered. I loved my years in high school.

College was great, too. I had the typical big university experience of leaving home to be independent for the first time and starting a new life with new friends. I went to the University of Illinois in Champaign-Urbana, so there were Big Ten football and basketball games, and I also joined a fraternity and spent a lot of time at the popular campus hang-outs. There always seemed to be some kind of special event or some festivities going on, and I always seemed to be in the middle of them.

Don't get me wrong. I also studied. My major was accounting, and University of Illinois was the number one school in the country for accounting at that time. It was a difficult major, but eventually I earned a bachelor's degree in accounting. That's when I realized that there was no way I could be an accountant for the rest of my life. I had no desire to be a CPA. So I drove south to Miami, Florida, and entered law school.

After graduating from the University of Miami School of Law, I was ready to be a trial lawyer. The first couple of law firms (two firms in two years) I tried, however, were not exactly my cup of tea, but then I landed on my feet at the law firm of Kubicki Draper in Miami. This firm was great because they paid well, the lawyers were top-notch, and they actually tried a lot of cases. In fact, I was trying civil cases at the age of twenty-six. I loved it. Overall, I tried about forty cases in eight years there, including several multi-million dollar cases. I learned that I was pretty good at it, too, as I lost only a handful of trials and won some really big ones. I was doing products liability, medical malpractice, and construction defect and automobile negligence cases, among others. In 2005, I passed the exam to become board certified in civil trial. I felt that this was definitely the career for me.

Around the same time I started working at Kubicki Draper, I joined an organization called Junior Chamber International (JCI), known as the Jaycees in the United States. JCI is an organization for young professionals who want to make a positive change in this world through community service, leadership development, and business networking. The local chapter I joined in Miami, the Coconut Grove Jaycees, was a perfect fit. It was a bunch of like-minded professionals who were really laid back. In 2001, I became president of the local organization and tripled the membership. We organized festivals, charity fundraisers, and networking events. We also conducted monthly projects to help foster kids, Alzheimer's patients, the homeless, poor children, and the needy. Our group was fantastic, and they re-elected me president in 2002.

We were so successful during that time that we won countless awards both inside and outside our international organization. We were recognized with awards from the City of Miami Mayor's Office, Easter Seals, the Miami Heart Research Institute, and United Way. We were also named the Most Outstanding Local Organization in the United States for 2001 and 2002. During both years, we were considered one of the most successful JCI organizations in the world.

These awards led to even more opportunities. I started getting invited to speak around the world on leadership and management. In addition to speeches, I developed leadership seminars to teach members of other JCI chapters how to attain the success we had in Miami. Between 2003 and 2007, I gave over 300 seminars and speeches across the United States and in many foreign countries. In 2006, I launched my own side-business in motivational speaking and leadership training. This was KnightVision Seminars, which was my company focusing on motivational speaking and business seminars. I had a passion for speaking and a real commitment to teaching other people how to develop their own leadership and management skills. Prior to the shooting, I had traveled to nineteen different states and twenty-four foreign countries as a speaker and trainer.

It wasn't all about trials and speaking engagements, however. In 2005, I met a young woman who was as beautiful on the inside as she was on the outside. I saw Lisa, with her dark hair and eyes and shining smile, for the first time at a JCI meeting, and we started dating in October, 2005. I knew right away that she was different from other women. She was sweet in a naïve sort of way. This was due in part to the fact that she had been sheltered for most of her life. Her main focus was her family, and after that, it was school and career. I was her first real boyfriend. When we started dating, everything seemed new to her and she enjoyed every minute of her life. Lisa and I quickly fell in love, and I knew this was the woman I had waited for all these years.

By March, 2006, I had already bought a ring. We were set to take a trip to Scotland, and my plan was to ask her to marry me in one of the castles in the Highlands. I had kept my plans a secret from everyone, including my parents and her parents, until the day before we were supposed to leave.

The night before we were to leave for Scotland, I drove to her parents' house to ask for her father's permission to marry his daughter. Although I had not met him yet, the killer was also at his parents' house that night but he was in his bedroom. I had no idea he was there until the next morning, when Lisa stopped by her parents' house to pick up a sweater from her mom before coming to my house to leave for the airport. What a mistake that was! Her evil and jealous brother started making fun of her, and then they got into an argument. To ruin her trip, ruin the surprise, and ruin the engagement, he told Lisa that I was going to ask her to marry me in Scotland. Her parents looked on in horror as he let out the secret I had carried for more than a month.

Undeterred, we went to Scotland and had a wonderful trip. Lisa told me what her brother had done so I wouldn't feel stupid, thinking she didn't know. But she waited until the second day because she wasn't sure if she should tell me or feign surprise. But she knew me, and she knew I wouldn't want to feel stupid. I value honesty a lot. That was the kind of relationship we had. We knew each other so well.

One year later, in February, 2007, Lisa and I were married in a beautiful ceremony at her church. The wedding was followed by a reception at the Deering Estate, which is an old Miami mansion that sits right on the bay with rows of palm trees lining the walkway from the house to the water. Lisa was Lebanese-American, so the reception had a Middle Eastern flair complete with *kibbeh* and *hummus* to eat and a belly dancer for entertainment.

One week before the wedding, I changed jobs. I wanted a job where I could still be in trial most of the time, but where I had more flexibility in my schedule so I could be a good family-man, too. I started working at Victor Rams & Associates, which was a firm that still did insurance defense litigation, but for only one insurance company (UAIC). My previous job had been a perfect fit during the earlier time in my life, and my new job was perfect for this new time in my life. I had a great boss who trusted me and allowed me to be quite autonomous. I was in a satellite office, so I was able to focus on my work and still have a lot of freedom. I continued to have success in trials, with multiple double-digit winning streaks. I was trying eight to ten cases a year and loving it. I had a secretary I completely relied on and who became a close friend in addition to being a coworker. The job also gave me the ability to attend my speaking engagements locally and in other countries. It was a perfect win-win situation for me and would only get better when I had a family, because then I would have time to be a good dad.

Over the next three years, between my work as a lawyer, my seminars, and my life with Lisa, I just felt that things couldn't get much better. Lisa and I loved to travel and we went on many wonderful trips. We went on a cruise to Hawaii with my family, and we went to Hungary, Italy, Turkey, and Estonia. Lisa joined me in Germany for the World Cup, and we also traveled to the Grand Canyon in Arizona. Life was wonderful.

In 2009, things got even better. If I could have counted my blessings, I don't think I would have finished counting in one day. My parents were healthy and happy. My two brothers were happily married and involved in my life. I won several big trials that year. I was a keynote speaker at the National Convention for Trial Court Administrators in Boston. So imagine my joy when Lisa got pregnant in 2009. We were so excited! I felt that my life would be complete as we started our family together.

Lisa wanted to tell everyone right away, but I told her that we should wait a few months to see how things worked out. I envisioned the look on my parents' faces when we would tell them that we would be giving them a grandchild.

I was so excited that I really didn't want to leave her before Thanksgiving, 2009, to attend a leadership conference in Tunisia, where I was slated to speak. I gave her a kiss good-bye and told her that I would be back soon. The event in Tunisia turned out to be better than I imagined. I spoke to 1,500 people. I finally felt like I had figured out how to connect with a large audience the same way I connected with participants in my seminar.

With my ten-day Tunisia trip behind me, I was thrilled to come home to Lisa and share the good news about my speech. I was concerned about how she felt, but she told me that everything was fine and showed me the latest ultrasound. This was three days before Thanksgiving, and I remember the feeling of contentment I had when Lisa greeted me that day at the airport.

At 5:00 p.m. on Thanksgiving, just hours before the shooting, Lisa and I called my parents to wish them a happy Thanksgiving. Dinner had not yet been served, so Lisa and I just walked into another room to call them. After Lisa spoke with my mom and dad, I got on the phone and told my mom about all the recent blessings in my life, including my speech in Tunisia and how I finally felt like I understood the art of speaking to a massive audience. The last words I said to my mom before the shooting were these: "Mom, I don't think my life can get any more blessed than this. Love you. Bye."

I realize that this chapter may seem ostentatious, but I want to clearly show how blessed my life was before the shooting. I always expected good things to happen to me. My father used to joke, in fact, that if I fell into a sewer, I would probably resurface holding a gold coin that I'd found on the bottom.

My history made it all the more difficult for me to deal with this tragedy because I had never experienced anything bad before. I had only tasted success and normalcy. I was not equipped for a major tragedy. I had never been in a situation requiring extensive recovery before.

And yet—everything I had spent a lifetime building was destroyed in a mere fifteen minutes. It was like the rug was pulled out from under my feet and I had fallen. Everything had been taken from me. It made no sense. Why, I kept asking myself, why did this happen? Was God sleeping? If not, where was he? Why let me taste such a blessed life and then let it be destroyed? Why did this happen when Lisa was pregnant? Why take these four people? Why? Why? Why?

During those first five weeks in the ICU, I was obsessed with these questions. I couldn't help myself. They filled my mind. To make matters worse, because I couldn't talk, I couldn't ask these questions out loud. Would I ever get answers?

I finally stopped asking why when I left the hospital. I figured I'd never get answers, so the best thing to do was just stop asking the questions. It took me weeks to figure that out, but that understanding helped me in the long run. In the meantime, I had to cope with my new reality.

Chapter Seven:

Learning to Cope

My mental state was fragile. I found it incredibly difficult to grieve for Lisa while trying to understand my own situation. There were two healing processes going on, one physical, the other, emotional. More than anything else, I wanted to go home. I wanted my old life back. I wanted everything to go back to the way it was before Thanksgiving. But I knew that even though I didn't want to accept it, this was my new reality.

Since I couldn't speak, I kept trying to mouth words to my parents, who did their best to make out what I was trying to tell them. I remember one day when I'd I had enough. Tears filling my eyes, I looked up at my mother. "I just want to go home," I said, or tried to say.

"Home?" she replied. "You want to go home? I know, sweetie. If I could pick you up in my arms right now and carry you out of here, I would do it right now."

Then my dad leaned over me. "Patrick," he said, "you just have to get a little stronger. Once you're a little stronger, if you want to get out of here, I'll take you myself."

Dealing with my situation was incredibly difficult. For the first two or three weeks, I could barely move. Not only could I not roll over, but I couldn't even slide myself up in the bed or shift my position, so I had bed sores on several parts of my body, including my head and buttocks. I could never get comfortable. The tubes sticking out of my chest, stomach, and torso were miserably uncomfortable. Days seemed to last forever and when I could stay awake, I was forever reassessing my situation and my memories. When I wasn't obsessively thinking, I was dozing off due to the mixture of drugs I was taking and my need for healing rest.

I couldn't do anything for myself. I was completely dependent on whoever was in the room with me. I know this feeling of helplessness can only be understood by someone else who has been in this position. So think about your dog. He can't eat unless you feed him. He can't go outside unless you open door for him. Maybe you have to carry him up the stairs or out to the car. When you leave, he's all by himself in the house until you return. The dog is completely dependent on you for his welfare. That's how I felt every day. But worse—I could hardly move. Your dog can stand up, walk around, sit down, change positions. I couldn't scratch an itch on my face. Even a dog can scratch.

Twice a day, nurses came in to wash me and change my bandages and sheets. Sounds simple, right? It's simple unless you're a 150-pound, helpless lump in the bed. (I had lost fifty pounds at that point). Two nurses would have to grab one side of the sheet, lift it, and roll me over to my side. Then they would push the clean sheets under me, come around to the other side, and roll me over the hump of dirty sheets to pull them out the other side. The tubes sticking out of my torso would get mashed into the bed. I could always feel them poking inside me. Sometimes my mouth and nose would end up pushed into the pillow so I couldn't breathe. I had little choice but to endure it. Twice a day, I would just try to get through the ordeal. There was really nothing I could do about it, and I couldn't even complain because I still couldn't talk. I still had the trach tube in my throat.

Next came the sponge bath. Sounds like every man's fantasy, right? Not even close! You have to remember that your only clothing is that flimsy hospital gown that is open down the back. If that doesn't humble a guy, just wait until sponge-bath time. Now the nurses were incredible, but this is generally what went down. First, they removed the gown, leaving me completely naked and vulnerable. Sometimes the nurse who was getting her cleaning supplies ready would suddenly realize that she had forgotten to bring in towels. "Be right back," she'd say. "Hang on. Don't move." And she would leave to get the towels.

And there I was, completely naked and spread-eagled on the hospital bed, bandages and tubes all over the place, with no way to rectify the situation. My weak little body looked like Mr. Burns from *The Simpsons*, and I was paler than I have ever seen in my life because I hadn't been outside in nearly four months. To make matters worse, every once in a while, another nurse or doctor would stroll in to take my blood or something, and all I could do is blink at them. Again, if this does not humble a person, I don't know what would.

Between the sponge baths, I generally entertained myself by watching television. This should have been a simple exercise, but it became another mission. The main problem with watching TV was that I could barely use the remote. I didn't have enough strength to even push the buttons on the remote, nor could I lift my head enough to see where the remote was on the bed, especially if I was lying half on it. My other senses quickly took over, thank goodness, and I was able to memorize where all the buttons were so I could change the channel.

But the main problem was that my wrists didn't work. While I was stuck in a coma for three months, my wrists fell asleep, too, and when I awoke, they stayed asleep. It's called radial nerve palsy, and, basically, my wrists just flopped around. I couldn't use my hands and fingers. The rehab therapists gave me braces to keep my wrists stiff, but with the braces, I didn't have the dexterity to press the buttons on the TV remote. And that made me cry. Television was all I had when my parents weren't in the room. It helped to keep my mind off of the bad thoughts piling up inside my head.

When the therapists saw my misery with the remote, they designed a more flexible wrist brace for my left hand that I could wear during the day so I could use the remote. I wore the stiff one only at night. So much effort to simply watch television overwhelmed me, but I was grateful to even have the distraction of the TV.

After the third week, when my parents came to visit, I had enough movement in my arms that I was able to use a communications board to "talk" to them. For more than two weeks, I'd only been able to nod or shake my head to answer questions. But now, we were going to try the communications board, which was a long, laminated sheet of paper with rows of letters on it. To "talk," I had to point to letters on it, and my parents called out the letters until I spelled the word I wanted. The letters were close together, and so were the rows, so with my almost useless muscles, it was not the easiest thing to use. Still, I was excited because this might work.

God bless my parents. Using the communications board was like playing Charades with blind people. They were so cute about it, and I know some of it was my fault, but the communications board was often frustrating. For starters, my wrists and fingers didn't work well, so it was hard for them to tell which letter I was pointing at. We were happy just to get the right letters, one at a time. If I was trying to "speak" a whole sentence, we sometimes got stuck on a common word for so long that my parents forgot the first words in the sentence. When they finally got the word, they'd celebrate, then turn to each other and ask, "What's he saying? What were the first five words again?"

Another problem was when a word had a double letter in it. For example, if I was spelling "street," here is how the exchange would go:

Mom: "S. T. R. E...."

I pointed to E again.

Mom: "I said E already."

I shook my head.

Mom: "Not E? What is it, then? A?"

I shook my head. I meant E. Double E. Why couldn't she understand? I kept pointing to E.

Mom: "Okay. E. That's what I thought." She turned to my father. "Earl, that's what I said, right?" Dad nodded. Mom turned back to me. "What's next?"

I pointed to the E again.

Mom: "It's not E? You shook your head, but it looks like you're pointing to E. Earl, come here and tell me what letter he's pointing at."

Imagine playing this game every day, several times a day. Sometimes we just gave up, but it never got me down. I got tired and a bit frustrated, but I loved them for even trying. It wasn't their fault. This double-letter confusion happened with everyone who tried to use the communications board with me. I wasn't able to use it well, which is what made it a tough task.

So unless it was really important, I just shrugged my shoulders and shook my head as well as I could. Just being able to communicate a little bit was enough. Having all those black thoughts and feelings bottled up inside me with no outlet was maddening, so I was thankful that my parents kept trying with me.

One of the worst physical things I had to cope with was the fungus in my lungs. I could feel it building up in there, and it made me cough a lot. Eventually, when they heard me coughing too much, the nurses came in and administered one of the most irritating procedures I had to endure. I had a hole in my throat where the trach tube was inserted and went down into my lungs. When I heard the nurses coming when I started to cough a lot, I tried my hardest to stop coughing. I knew what was coming next, and it was not pleasant. First, the nurse would lean close to my mouth and ask if I was wheezing. I always shook my head, but they never believed me because they could hear me wheezing. And then, of course, a little cough would slip out.

Nurse: "Steven, do you think we need to clean out your lungs?"

Me: *No!* I shook my head as violently as I could.

Nurse: "I think we should clean you out a bit."

I don't know how big the thing was that she would stick into the tube and down into my lungs, but it seemed to be the size of a very long drinking straw. After sticking it down the tube, she rattled it around in my lungs to try and break up the mucous. Imagine what it feels like to have someone rattle a glass stick around inside your lungs. Instantly, I would begin coughing so deeply and violently that green stuff came spewing out of my mouth. Several times it landed on the opposite wall, seven feet away. That's how violently the stick in my lungs made me cough. Even worse, the procedure always was done two or three times in a row. Each time, they asked me the same question.

Nurse: "Steven, do you think we got it all, or should we do it again?"

Me: *Yes!* This time I nodded my head as emphatically as I could. *Yes, you got it all.*

Nurse: "Really, Steven? It sounds to me like you're still wheezing. Let's do it again."

Why ask me if you're just going to keep torturing me? I hated that procedure. It ranked second in pain only behind that other procedure where they had stuck the tube up my nose and down my throat and all the way down to my intestines. I hope that I never have to endure either procedure ever again.

One day, a nurse rattled that stick around my lungs so hard I cried for an hour. I knew she was just doing her job, but I just couldn't take it anymore. These were my daily routines in the first several weeks. I had just about reached my limit.

Whenever I stopped focusing on my painful body, however, I started crying again. How could I not think about Lisa? Grieving is hard to go through when there are no other complications, but my physical state made it almost impossible. It seemed like I had only two choices: lament my physical state or grieve over my deceased wife. What terrible options! I was not equipped to deal with either one, but there seemed to be no alternative.

Just when I'd start to feel a little acceptance of the fact that I could hardly move, I would remember Lisa and get hit with a wave of despair and depression. The tears would flow uncontrollably, and there was nothing anyone could do to console me. When I could finally calm myself down about Lisa, one of my tubes would pinch me or I would start to cough. It was a vicious cycle.

To make matters worse, the shooting sometimes began replaying in my head as if it was on an endless loop. The doctors later told me that I had Post Traumatic Stress Disorder (PTSD), which is very common among victims of tragedy. Soldiers often suffer from PTSD after returning from battle. It works like this: the tragic incident replays in your head from start to finish, and each time it does, you actually feel the same anxiety and apprehension you experienced the first time. It's as though you're there again. It was bad enough that I had to live through being shot once, but now my brain was tricking me into thinking that I was actually experiencing the shooting again and again and again.

First, the killer's image would come into my mind. I would see his face and see the gun being pointed at my head. Next came the sounds of the gunshots. *BANG. BANG. BANG.* I could feel my ears ringing again. It seemed to be happening right there in my hospital room. *BANG. BANG. BANG.*

My body would wrench, my arms and legs would twitch, I would turn my head and close my eyes. I just wanted it to stop. I would feel the searing pain in my stomach and hear the silence after the shooting ended.

The next image in my head would be the blood spilling out of my stomach. Even though I was lying in the hospital, I was sure I was dying.

Next, I would see Carla lying on the floor, groaning and then becoming silent. Finally came the absolute silence. Even with all of the whirring and beeping machines around my bed, my mind took me into that total, tomb-like silence. There was nothing I could do about it. I would relive the arrival of the paramedics, the helicopter ride. I would slide into the ER again. And just when the story was ending, it would start all over again. *BANG. BANG. BANG.*

Can you imagine it?

I was crying every day, sometimes every hour. I couldn't keep my emotions in check. I cried over Lisa. I cried because she was pregnant. I cried over the six-year-old girl he shot. I cried over my present situation. I wondered what the future might hold and cried some more. Every time the tragedy replayed in my mind, I cried.

Can you imagine it?

The only thing I could do was to pray for strength. I was pretty pragmatic about those prayers. I was asking God to just give me enough strength to make it until my folks arrived in the afternoon. At night, I was praying that he would just give me the strength to make it through one more night. I knew this was a normal process, that my timeframes did not matter, that things would get better in his time. I had to trust that God had a plan for me. Who was I to question the details of that plan? Nevertheless, even though I trusted God's plan, I struggled every day to keep moving forward.

Nighttime was the worst. My parents left when visiting hours ended, and the nurses' visits were less frequent at night so I had a chance to sleep a bit. But I was lonely. I felt too weak mentally to deal with the nighttime emptiness.

When I couldn't sleep, I watched infomercials on TV. I think I saw every one ever made, and I actually was ready to buy one particularly fancy blender when I got out of the hospital. The reality, of course, was that I hated nights. Mostly, I spent my nights just praying for enough strength to get through that night.

My parents saw my fear of being alone at night in one moment of uncontrollable emotion on my part. Visiting hours were 1 p.m. to 6 p.m., then again from 8 p.m. to 9 p.m. Every day, my parents came in early, left for dinner, and came back. One night, however, they were unusually tired, and when the early visiting hours ended, my mom gave me a kiss and told me that she and my father weren't coming back that night. She told me they would see me the next day at one o'clock. They'd been spending endless hours in my hospital room. I nodded to her that I understood.

But then my lips then started quivering and the tears started streaming down my face. I couldn't hide my emotions very well that day. My mother instantly reversed course and told me that they would be back at eight o'clock. She begged me to stop crying, and then she came over to stroke my hair. Thanks to her gentle caress, I mustered up the strength to stop crying. This little episode showed how fragile I was every moment of the day

I kept trying to be strong, but I was at my emotional breaking point. All I could do was pray every day and every night for God to give me more strength. I prayed, and then I tried to get through to the next event: breakfast, morning bath, give-blood time, lunch, change-sheets time, visiting hours, dinner, visiting hours, bedtime, wake-up time. I just wanted to make it from event to event with my sanity more or less intact. I prayed for strength and I trusted God to get me there.

Chapter Eight:

No More Pity-Parties

By the third week after I woke up, I was still an emotional wreck. The grieving and suffering lasted for months, but in those first few weeks, I had become the world's expert at throwing pity-parties for myself. I had it down to a science. I could take any thought and lead myself down the path of self-pity and depression.

It wasn't hard to do. As I said before, the shooting was replaying over and over in my head, so I always had to deal with the PTSD symptoms anyway. Every time I thought about my medical situation or looked at all the tubes sticking out of me, that made me more miserable and frustrated. Now add in the constant beeping of the machines and my inability to move, and you start to have a perfect recipe for a pity-party. For the ultimate cherry on top, all I had to do was think about Lisa and the others that died on that day. My thoughts were succinct: *Life sucks!*

This process of negative thinking leading to near depression is very interesting to me now, two years later.

I can see how there was a snowball effect, where one negative thought leads to the next until the burden of negativity becomes overwhelming. If it happened to you, you'd crack, too.

I can also imagine how people who deal with catastrophic loss and tragedy may have more than they can handle, from injury and pain to financial ruin to the loss of a loved one. It can be difficult to ever pull yourself out of the hole. But one day I reminded myself of a quote I'd used in a speech back in 2003: Always remember the First Rule of Holes. *When you are in one, stop digging!*

There I was, lying in the hospital bed, unable to move or talk. That was a pretty deep hole. It didn't help that everyone from the nurses to my family were treating me with kid gloves. That was digging the hole deeper. I had PTSD, which dug the hole deeper with every replay of the shooting.

I don't profess to know exactly how to deal with someone else in my situation, but anyone who came near me in those first weeks showed unbelievable compassion and sympathy for me. They were worried about me. They cared about me. Nobody knew what to say to me, and there were a lot of tears shed in my room in the ICU. That was nice, but it also allowed me to wallow in my deepening hole of despair. My thoughts vacillated between confusion, grief, anger, and fear. I worked myself into depression with this pattern of thinking. *My situation has to be the worst one in this hospital. I can only imagine what these other people are thinking in their rooms. They think they have it so bad. Well, they don't have it as bad as I do. I dare them to come in here and tell me how bad their injury or tragedy or loss is and compare it with mine. I dare them!*

One day, however, things changed. A new blessing came into my life. It was no coincidence that we crossed paths because he was very clearly sent to me from above. He didn't come strutting into my room ready to change me. In fact, he didn't walk into my room at all. One day, a young black man named Alfredo Bless came rolling into my room on his wheelchair. He had a smile that started at one ear and went all the way to the other. All teeth. Pure joy.

Alfredo introduced himself to me and then to my parents, who were there. The nurses already knew him because he was a volunteer at the hospital, the guy who came down and visited the worst patients in the ICU to try and give them encouragement to keep moving forward. God's love flows from Alfredo Bless, and if you cannot see it, he will certainly tell you that this is where his joy comes from.

Since he was in a wheelchair and I was lying flat on my back, he was the only person I didn't have to look up to see. With my minimal ability to move, I could barely turn my head to look at this man who was smiling so passionately at me. He said a few pleasant things to me, gave me some encouraging words, and then started in on the serious stuff. First, he started talking about some of the tubes that were still sticking out of me. He described my aches, pains, and frustrations perfectly. He told me what to expect with the feeding tubes, and he sympathized with my plight of completely atrophied muscles.

This guy has obviously been where I am, I said to myself, *because he knows way too much about what I am going through.* I couldn't speak. I could barely nod. But the intense piercing stare I was giving him, let him know he had my attention.

He went on. He, too, had been shot in a violent crime. He, too, was an innocent victim. He, too, had been in the wrong place at the wrong time. He described his recovery. And then he started to tell me what the immediate future would hold for me in the next few weeks in the ICU. This helped me a lot. It made me start looking forward, toward recovery, rather than backward, at the incident.

After Alfredo went through all the various situations I would encounter in the future, he looked at my legs and got serious. "I can see that you can't move," he said. "Don't worry, bro. You'll get used to it, and you can be very functional even when you're paralyzed. Just look at me."

At that, my mom chimed in. "Oh, he's not paralyzed," she said. "His muscles are just very weak and he can't move right now, but that will all come back."

Alfredo's expression changed from serious to pure elation. "What? You're not paralyzed? You're gonna walk again? That's great, see, because my legs, they're on strike, but you, bro, you're gonna walk again. That's wonderful!"

He gave me a huge smile. I wish I could have reacted better, but at the time, I could barely put on a normal size smile. Inside, however, I felt an immediate change. Here was a guy who had it much worse than me.

Yes, we were both shot, but he was paralyzed from the waist down. I'd be back on my feet eventually, but he was stuck for the rest of his life in a wheelchair. He spent his time visiting the worst of the worst patients in the ICU. And there he was, smiling nonstop. He had a joy in his heart that most people don't have even in their best times.

Alfredo came to visit me once or twice a week after that, and each time I tried to show him that I had a renewed positive energy. I began to focus on my recovery and the possibilities for the future. I stopped digging the hole.

As my parents also noticed a difference in me, they encouraged my new attitude. Day after day, they began telling me stories about other people in the ICU. I began to understand that there were people that had it much worse than I did.

A girl in the room next to me had fallen off a horse, landed on her head, and suffered a massive head injury. It was so bad, the doctors didn't think she would ever be fully functional again. She was not quite a vegetable, but she was non-responsive. My parents told me how her family would try to talk to her or get her to swallow a pill, how she just lay there drooling. I overheard my parents ask the nurses about it, and they said the prognosis was not favorable.

A guy came in after being shot eight or nine in his torso. My parents thought he might have been a gang member because there were about ten other young men in the waiting room wearing the same color bandana. They were going in two at a time to visit their friend. He, too, had an unfavorable prognosis. He was fighting for his life every day.

Then things got worse in the ICU. On January 12, a 7.0 magnitude earthquake struck in Haiti, destroying nearly every building in the capital city and killing thousands of people. Many of those who did survive were shipped to the United States for treatment in hospitals in South Florida. Quite a few of them ended up coming into my ICU. Their stories weren't identical, but they were similar and typically sounded like this: A young Haitian woman lost her husband when their home collapsed. Their three children were missing. She had no contact with any of her extended family members. A roof had fallen on her, crushing her legs, and she could not walk. She woke up to find herself in a hospital in a foreign country where everyone spoke English, not Creole.

Hearing these stories day after day certainly changed my mindset: *I'm in the best shape of anyone in this ICU*, I finally said to myself. *Wow, I feel bad for these people. I am so blessed to be on the road to recovery. My prognosis is good. I will probably walk again. I don't have any major brain damage. My family is right here with me. I have a lot of friends, and I'm sure that I will someday go back to being a lawyer. I'm thankful to live in the United States. I appreciate the nurses and doctors in this ICU. Compared to everyone else here, I have things pretty darn good.*

I also thought about how lucky I was to have such an amazing family to support me through this process. Not only my parents, but my brothers were also very active in visiting me and making me feel like I could get through it. My brother Kerry and his wife Beth came down from Chicago three times (twice while I was sleeping). He saved the ICU stickers to show me he'd been there. My other brother, Brian, and his wife Nikki live in South Florida and came in at least once a week after I woke up to give me encouragement. I'll never forget asking Brian to rub my legs because they were so sore. He looked at me like I was joking at first, but when he saw the miserable look on my face, he immediately took to rubbing my legs. He massaged my legs for twenty minutes. This unwavering support from my family was essential in my recovery.

It started with Alfredo Bless, my parents, and my brothers. It continued with the hospital chaplain, Cathy Kino, who came in and prayed with me every time she was at the hospital. She looked like an angel and was clearly filled with God's spirit. She gave me hope and prayed that God would give me strength.

My hope and faith were multiplied by the attitudes of the nurses who cared for me each day, and I kept gaining momentum as I heard each new story in the ICU. This was the end of my pity-parties and the beginning of my new reality. I was determined to be positive from this point on. I was determined to focus on the future.

After I left the hospital, I began telling people about Alfredo Bless and the end of my pity-parties. A short time after I returned home, someone sent an email to me with the story below. I don't know the origin of the story, but I think it perfectly sums my thoughts.

The Cross You Bear

Gladys had seen some hard times in her life and was coping with a great deal of loss. At times, her burdens appeared overwhelming and she started to lose hope. One day, in a moment of despair she cried out, "Dear God, I can't take it anymore. This is more than I can handle. Please lighten my load."

The clouds parted above her, and a heavenly figure appeared and said to her, "Everyone must carry a cross, Gladys, but your prayer was heard, so I will remove yours now and allow you to choose another cross to carry. Just enter that field over there, lay down your cross, and go pick out your new cross."

Gladys walked over to the field and saw crosses everywhere. There must have been a thousand of them. The crosses appeared in all sizes, and some were astoundingly large. One cross was so large that the top of it was hidden by the clouds above. Gladys carefully walked through the crosses, surveying the entire field, searching for one cross that she could comfortably bear.

At last, she found what she was looking for. It was a cross so tiny that she almost overlooked it. Fortunately, it was glistening in the sun and it caught her attention. "This is it!" she exclaimed. "This is the cross I want to carry."

And just at that moment, the heavenly spirit reappeared and said, "But, Gladys, that is the same cross you were carrying before."

Chapter Nine:

Celebrating Every Small Victory

Once I freed myself from the shackles of the pity-parties, my old zest for life started to come back. As I started to feel more positive about my potential for recovery, I decided to celebrate every victory along the way, no matter how small. My parents were a big help in this regard because they were my biggest cheerleaders and cheered whenever any positive news came my way. We celebrated when each tube was removed, when a machine was taken out of the room, when I could move my arm just a little more. Nothing was off-limits, and our cheering turned the atmosphere in the room into a positive vibe that could be felt by anyone who came in. I was all for it because celebrating was a lot better than crying.

My mother got all chipper any time she heard something good from the nurses, and she always told me the news with a twinkle in her eye that made me excited, too. My father took it to another level. Every day they came to visit, the hospital printed a new guest pass sticker to give them access to the ICU. My dad saved every sticker and wrote notes on them about what great new thing had happened that day. It became a little game among us to figure out something positive and exciting to write on today's sticker. Sometimes my mother would be telling us something and he would say, "Hold on, I want to write that down on the sticker."

It still wasn't easy for me. I still couldn't speak, but we were getting better at using the communication board. One day, they came in and I nodded my head and looked down at my side. Then I spelled out "tube" on the communication board. A quick game of guess-the-word followed.

My mother: "A tube? You need a tube? There's a problem with the tube? I don't see a tube there. There was a tube there? The tube is gone?" She turned to my father. "Earl, they took the tube out of the right side of his chest today! You can see the hole there where they removed it." Back to me: "That's fantastic. Did it hurt?"

My dad: "Hold on, I need to write this down on my sticker."

If you ever met my parents, you'd see how cute this little exchange was. It shows the kind of positive energy and constant celebration that helped me get through those incredibly difficult times with an optimistic eye on recovery. I knew there was a possibility that I might not fully recover. After all, at this point, one month after I woke up, I still could hardly move and I certainly couldn't talk.

But I was already developing the mindset that whatever my new future held, whatever my new reality was, I would be okay with that and would enjoy life with the same zest as ever. Every time they walked in and noticed that another machine was gone, I received a recap of all the machines that had been in my room. My parents told me about the breathing machines, the heart monitors, the blood pressure monitors, the machines that watched for excessive coughing or restricted breathing, the dialysis machines, the feeding bags, the fluid bags, the IV tubes. All of them, one by one, being taken away. They were excited about my progress, and their attitude made me excited.

I began to regain some movement in my arms as the muscles began to wake up and develop. It was slow going. I think I gained maybe two inches of movement per day, and I made mental notes on how far I had moved my arm the day before.

You cannot imagine the frustration of having an itch on your nose, but when you instinctively go to scratch it, you're barely strong enough to lift your arm half way to your face. But I was patient. Instead of lamenting my inability to touch my face, I focused on my ability to move my arm two inches more than the previous day.

Think about how often you touch your face. You rub your eyes when you're sleepy. You touch your cheeks or mouth or nose. If you have an itch, you scratch it. Just pay attention as to how often you touch your face in a given day. Now imagine the immense pleasure I received on the very first day I was strong enough to get my hand all the way to my face. This happened three weeks after I woke up. I knew I had been getting close, but one morning, I woke up and just lifted my arm and it kept going and going. When my hand touched my face, I felt like crying. I just left my hand on my face, slowly moving it up and down my face, across my cheeks, over my nose, around my eyes. I felt as though I had been given a very special present that day. I knew I would never take anything for granted again.

As movement began to return in my arms and legs, I used every waking moment to build muscle in my extremities and remind myself how to move. It's amazing how much your muscles forget when they go to sleep for three months. Eventually, I was able to bend my legs and even raise my arms up all the way over my head. It was funny because I didn't have great range of motion, but there I was, waving my arms around, lifting them up and down, doing arm circles, moving my legs. In the beginning, nurses came running in as though I was flagging them down. Then they just smiled. "Are you just exercising again?"

My parents, of course, were great cheerleaders. In our parents' eyes, we never stop being the little boy or girl they raised from infancy. My parents still look at me like everything I do is the greatest thing in the world. It's just like when I took my first steps as a toddler, or the first time I used the toilet all by myself. As long as I was in the hospital, they were so proud of me and cheered me on at every step in my recovery. For example, once my dad realized that I could actually raise my arms up all the way over my head, he got so excited he asked me to do it over and over. He used that voice people use when they talk to their babies or their dogs. We both got excited when I actually raised my hands. I actually felt like I was doing something incredible.

Dad: "There's my boy! Let me see you raise those arms up over your head."

I immediately lift them, but my wrists are still flopping around.

Dad: "All right! That's so great. Let me see you do it again."

I raise them again.

Dad: "Look at that! Where's a pen? I have to write this down on my sticker."

In the same way, my mother got excited when I started to move my legs. She asked me to lift my feet off the bed and put them back down. She asked me to lift them back up again. To her, it was an amazing feat of strength. I guess it was a bit of a shock to them, considering that just three weeks earlier, I couldn't move at all and that my legs looked like little sticks with no muscle on them.

Eventually, I was able to move my legs in a little bit of a bicycle motion, and thereafter when my mom came in, she asked me to show her how I could pedal. It was a struggle, but I managed to lift my legs and pedal a make-believe bicycle as well as I could. We were truly celebrating every little victory with any kind of movement.

Every day, I was dreaming about having water in my mouth. Because of the hole in my stomach, they were feeding me through the tube that went in my nose, bypassed my stomach, and went to my intestines. They couldn't put water in my mouth for fear that I would swallow it, which might have caused complications in the healing process in my stomach. But every day, I asked for water, and every day, they told me I couldn't have any. After four months, my mouth was so dry it felt like I had a mouth full of sand. I just wanted to wet my tongue for one minute.

Finally, as my stomach began to heal a bit, a nurse took pity on me. As I went through my daily routine of mouthing to her that I wanted water, I expected her to tell me no. Instead, she told me to hang on for one second. She went out and she came back with one small ice chip. She told me not to swallow. Then she put the ice chip on my tongue and said to just let it melt in my mouth. It was pure bliss.

I don't generally prefer to drink plain water, but when you cannot have water for four months, it tastes like a party in your mouth. Even now as I write this, I can vividly remember the feeling of that ice chip melting in my dry, parched mouth. Eventually, of course, the ice chips weren't enough. I wanted something with taste to it. The nurses, however, were still telling me that I couldn't drink anything because there was still a tiny hole in my stomach. Just for what I assume was pure torture, they asked me what I would like to drink if I could drink it. I mouthed to them that I wanted Gatorade Fruit Punch. They smiled and told me I could have it "soon enough."

And then one day, a nurse came in and told me that she was going to give me a treat. She took out a tiny sponge on a stick and dipped it into a small bottle of Gatorade Fruit Punch. She gave me very clear instructions about using the sponge to wet my lips and just give me a taste of the drink without any of it actually getting into my mouth. She was afraid I would swallow it. I nodded that I understood and then touched that sponge to my lips. I felt like a kid on Christmas Eve. I felt goose bumps all over my body. That little processed fruit taste of Gatorade was magnificent. The water was pure bliss, but this stuff was like a drug. I wanted more. My instincts took over. I opened my mouth and clamped onto the sponge. She tried to pull it out and told me to stop, but I sucked every last drop out of the sponge while I held the stick with my teeth. She didn't do the sponge thing again for a few days, but it was okay by then because my stomach had healed and I could have all the Gatorade Fruit Punch I wanted.

It seemed like every few days, we were celebrating the removal of either another machine or another of the many tubes sticking out of my body. With each machine being removed, it would become a little quieter at night, which allowed me to sleep better. With each tube that was pulled out, I felt a little more comfortable.

Sometimes, the doctor would simply pull a tube out of my chest, and it would make a popping sound. That usually wasn't painful, but sometimes it was unbearable. If anyone ever tells you that pulling out a catheter is only going to cause "mild discomfort," they're lying. Take it from me. Pain aside, any tube coming out of my body was a victory.

Day by day, we found new victories to celebrate. But I was still unable to speak. I had so many things going through my mind, and I couldn't wait to tell someone what I was thinking. One day when the nurses and doctors came in to see me, I overheard them talking about getting me to speak. Would I soon have one more victory to celebrate?

Chapter Ten:

Tears Turn into Words

There is nothing worse that you can do to a lawyer than take away his ability to speak. For three months, I was in a coma and silent, and then for another four weeks, I was awake but could barely communicate. There were so many words piled up inside me, I thought I was going to explode. Without a doubt, the biggest "tube" victory was when they pulled the tracheotomy tube out of my throat. We were all nervous. I had not said a word in four months. Would I be able to talk?

My brother Kerry and his family had come down from Chicago to see me the morning before they removed the trach tube. In typical fashion, we played our frustrating game of their trying to read my lips and my using the communications board. Just imagine trying to communicate with seven people in the room when they're all trying to guess what you're mouthing or what letter you're pointing to on the board.

When the doctor pulled out my tracheotomy tube and asked me to say something, I was scared. Really scared. What if no sound came out? What if I was unable to form words? I took a deep breath, sent a quick prayer up to God for strength, and then opened my mouth. "Hello." The voice I heard was deep and husky, and the word coming out of my mouth didn't sound quite right. I knew it would take a while for me to get the hang of talking again.

But when I looked at the doctor and my parents, they looked like I had just given the greatest oration ever heard on earth. Their eyes widened and their mouths opened with delight. Both my parents had tears in their eyes. I could see that this was a really big deal for everyone in the room.

Now if you're a lawyer and professional speaker, what do you do after you haven't been able to talk for four months? You talk, of course. As much as you can. I know they couldn't understand most of what I said that day because a lot of it was just noise and sounds. But I was talking! And no one was going to ever be able to shut me up again. For the rest of the day, I practiced making vowel sounds and consonant sounds. Every time a nurse came in to my room, I waited until she got really close to me, and then I said, as loudly as I could, "Thank you for everything you have done for me." Each time, the response was incredible. The nurses looked at me with wide eyes, smiled, and hugged me.

I practiced speaking for two days. I was trying to get my mouth used to saying words again. When Kerry came back two days later, I was able to speak to him and his family. When my other brother, Brian, came in, I couldn't wait to say a few words to him, too. I could talk! This felt like the greatest gift God had ever given to me. I was finally telling people what was going on in my head. At each step of the healing process, I celebrated another victory. Moving my arms felt great, and water tasted even better, but being able to talk again after more than four months of silence was one of the top moments in my life.

There was one more thing that I was really looking forward to. I knew it was right around the corner. The doctors had been talking for days about the fact that my stomach appeared to have healed. Maybe I could try a liquid diet. I was happy to think of any event that involved pulling that tube out of my nose and putting something into my mouth. The feeding tube came out a day later, and they brought me various liquid meals. I had smoothies, pureed vegetables, and some corn soup. None of it tasted particularly good, but I was thrilled nonetheless to feel liquid in my mouth. They monitored me for several days after each liquid meal, and my body responded positively each time.

And then I quickly learned that I had a new problem to deal with. That was something I couldn't believe how difficult it was to relearn. Since my muscles had atrophied and I hadn't used any muscles in my throat for almost four months, I had forgotten how to swallow. I'd always taken swallowing for granted. It was an effortless task. But now? I couldn't get the hang of it. The nurses gave me various techniques to relearn how to swallow, but nothing worked. Most of the time, those liquid meals just ran down my throat, but if there were any chunks, the chunks got stuck in my throat and I had to cough them out.

This process of relearning how to swallow was getting extremely frustrating until a therapist came to my room and taught me how to pull my tongue back toward the rear of my throat and push my Adam's apple forward and up to simulate the motion of swallowing.

I worked on this for a week before I finally got it. Twice I got something stuck in there, where the oxygen flow was blocked, and I started to choke. Choking causes immediate panic, of course, and one time I was sure I would never be able to get that little piece of food out of my throat. I was all alone, and I just kept coughing until it finally came back up. In the end, of course, I did relearn how to swallow. That was another event to be celebrated.

And then the day arrived where the doctor said that I could have anything I wanted to eat. My family was ready to go out and get whatever feast I wanted. I thought about pizza, but I went with a cheeseburger and french fries from McDonalds. As soon as my brother Brian walked into the room with those fragrant bags from McDonalds, my mouth started to water. I was so excited to eat real food and even more excited to indulge in a hamburger and fries. Brian unwrapped the burger for me and poured the fries out onto the wrapper. I picked it up as well as I could with my useless wrists and took a bite of the burger. It exploded in my mouth with greasy goodness. I ate four french fries, and then I pushed the food away and sat back against my pillows.

Brian: "What's wrong? Does it taste bad?"

Me: "I am so full, I can't eat another bite."

Yes, too full. One thing I hadn't calculated was how

small my stomach had become after four months with nothing in it. In those first few months after I woke up, I couldn't eat more than a few bites of anything before I became extremely full. My eyes were certainly bigger than my stomach. Each day, I would anticipate eating something, only to be full after barely tasting it.

But that didn't stop me from ordering anything and everything from every restaurant I could think of. I had pizza on day two, then bowls of fruit for breakfast, and Chinese food for lunch. It was like the water and my ability to talk. We don't appreciate ordinary things like food until they're taken away and we cannot have them. I will never take anything for granted again.

On days when I felt down or depressed, there was always someone there to cheer me up. Sometimes, it was my parents or brothers, other times it was Alfredo or Chaplain Cathy. But what truly amazed me was how much the nurses and technicians cared about their jobs. I was not just another body to them. They didn't treat me like a job. Instead, they felt true compassion for me and were always trying to make me feel better. For ex-ample, one of the ICU staff, a guy named Rich, often came in just to give me a hug and make sure I was doing okay. Another ICU guy, Mounir, came to visit me even when I was on a different floor from his assigned room. He just hung out for a little while and treated me like a normal guy. Then there was the day that I was cry-ing profusely, and a nurse named Amber came in and asked if a foot rub would help make me feel better. Who would turn that down? My point is that these people touched me with their compassion in ways that made me want to keep going and celebrate each small victory. For their kindnesses, I am eternally grateful.

Day by day, I gained more strength. Soon I could sit up. One day the physical therapist asked me if I would like to try standing up. I didn't think I would be able to do that, but I told her that I'd give it a try. So this little female therapist tells me not to worry, but that she is about to violate me. She was joking, of course, but because I had almost no muscles that worked, no coordination, she was going to have to grab my buttocks and pull me in tight to her to lift me off the bed with the lifting belt. We laughed about the idea of being violated and I sat on the edge of the bed with my feet dangling down. She positioned herself in front of me, between my legs. Then she wrapped her belt around my back and placed her hands firmly on my buttocks. She counted to three and then lifted me up. Well, my body just flopped toward her, and my arms landed on her shoulders holding on for dear life. My legs could not support me. So she pulled me really tight into her chest.

"Doesn't this feel great?" she asked. "You're standing!"

We laughed again. In any other situation, this kind of full body-to-body contact would be alarmingly inappropriate, but I was elated just to be vertical. My verticality lasted about twenty-five seconds before I got dizzy and my blood pressure spiked. She promptly laid me back down on the bed and I lay there, looking up at the ceiling with a wide smile on my face, celebrating one more victory.

As my ability to talk improved and people could understand me better, all I wanted to do was make phone calls to anyone and everyone in my phone's address book. I called my secretary, who had been very concerned about me. She was so happy to hear from me, and it was good for me to hear another friendly voice. One of my first questions to her was "Who is handling my legal cases?"

I called other friends, too, people I knew would be excited to hear my voice. One of the best calls I made was to my friend Arrey, who works at JCI World Headquarters. I think he was stunned to see my name appear on his cell phone as the caller, but when he answered, I went right to the point.

"Arrey," I said, "I'm still recovering, and I can't even stand yet, but if you haven't given away my slot as a speaker at the JCI World Congress in Osaka, Japan, in November, it is still my intention to walk out on stage and speak." I was asking this question in April. I had been talking for one week.

He didn't even hesitate. "Patrick, I wouldn't have dreamed of anyone else doing the morning show. We were just waiting for you to wake-up."

It was then that I realized that I wasn't the only one celebrating every one of my small victories. I had friends, coworkers, and other family members who were following my progress every step of the way. In the months after I left the hospital, they all told me that they'd always been holding out some sliver of hope for me, even when I was in my worst moments. They told me that every time they received a text message from my brother that something positive had happened, they celebrated with me. Learning about these connections gave me even more resolve to move forward and get better. I wasn't celebrating alone. I had my parents, my family, and all my friends celebrating with me. Like Arrey, they were just waiting for me to wake up.

Chapter Eleven:

Positive Energy Returns

As positive as I might have been on any given day, my new reality was still pretty negative. Here we were now, five weeks after I woke up, and I still had very little strength. I couldn't sit up on my own, and even when they tried to sit me up, it took the efforts of one therapist kneeling at my back to push me up and another therapist in front trying to pull me up. After thirty seconds of this level of effort, I got dizzy and my blood pressure spiked so high they laid me right back down. I still couldn't even roll myself over in bed without assistance. Even when the therapist tried standing me up that one time, I had to lie back down instantly.

In that fifth week after I woke up, they started transferring me from the bed to a hospital chair so that I could let my body get used to the feeling of sitting in a chair again. This chair was like a dentist chair, where I was slightly reclined and there were supports for my legs. They slid me over from the bed to the recliner using a board, and then they slowly raised the back of the chair to a slightly straighter position. It was a struggle each time because my body had been flat for over four months. My muscles, my organs, and my blood flow had not had to fight against gravity for that entire time. Whenever my body was even slightly erect, I got woozy and overly tired.

To add to the struggle, I still had bed sores from being immobile for so long. My inner organs had been so delicate, and my neurovascular system so fragile, that the nurses and doctors rarely moved me while I was in the coma. This resulted in bed sores that led to open, cracked wounds on my head, my back, my shoulders, and my buttocks. By the time I was trying to sit in the chair, most of the bed sores had healed, but guess where the final sore remained. It was right under my tailbone. I had to sit on it.

The therapists and nurses really tried to help me out. They let me sit on two pillows. They tried to let me lie flat enough in the recliner to ease the direct pressure on this sore. But the pain was still excruciating. Every day, I had to come up with new ways to distract my brain for a few minutes. Mostly, I focused on beating my time from the day before. Again, this is where my parents came in handy because they got so excited every time I told them I had set a new endurance record. In a much smaller way, think of it like when you're on the treadmill and you try to just go for five minutes longer than the day before. Those five minutes can seem like an eternity. That's how it was for me, too.

I remember sitting there, trying to make a game out of it. I tried to tell myself stories in my mind. Or I tried to watch a television program and do everything possible not to look at the clock. I envisioned myself telling my parents about my new record. That always motivated me to go longer. When the pain from the sore got too bad, I tried to lift myself up maybe an inch, using the little physical strength I had. I had a goal. I was going to make it.

One day, when I was trying to kill some time, I told the therapist that I was planning on going to Osaka, Japan, in November to speak at the JCI World Congress. We then started talking about the various topics of my seminars and workshops. Inevitably, she saw that most of my seminars have an element of positive-thinking in them. She was especially intrigued with my seminar called Positive Seduction: Getting Others to Follow You Willingly. I am very passionate about my seminars, and as I began to speak to her about the seminar, I really started to feel like my old self. I knew she could feel it, too. My guess is that she probably regretted asking me about the seminar because I gave her a thirty-minute, abbreviated version of it and never paused to give her a chance to cut me short. The positive energy was returning inside me. I knew that could only be a good thing. To top it off, that half hour distraction allowed me to set a new record for sitting in my chair. I was definitely going in the right direction.

Three days before I was to be transferred from the hospital to a rehabilitation facility in Miami, a therapist came in and asked me if I felt like I could sit up long enough to go somewhere in a wheel chair. Then she told my parents that if I could handle it, they could take me outside.

I was so excited I nearly jumped out of bed. Well...
I was excited until I remembered that I still couldn't
move by myself. I hadn't seen sunlight in over four
months. I have never seen my skin so pale, and all I'd
had to look at for the five weeks after I woke up were
my television set and the bluish-green walls of my hospital room.

The therapist sat me up on the edge of the bed
with my feet dangling down. First, I had to get my blood
pressure to stabilize so I wouldn't get woozy. Then she
used her lifting belt and lifted me out of the bed and
into a wheelchair. I felt like a kid on his way to a toy
store! I was beaming as my parents rolled me through
the hallways to the front door. All of the nurses were
encouraging me on the way out with smiles and well
wishes. The anticipation was almost overwhelming.

When we finally rolled outside, I was instantly hit
with the smell of fresh air and the feel of a nice spring
breeze on my skin. I was outside, and it was wonderful.
The sun was too bright for my eyes, however, so my
parents moved me into the shade of a tree. They were
concerned about the sunlight being too much for me
and kept offering to take me back inside, but I refused. I
just wanted to enjoy the moment for as long as I could.
There I sat, listening to the birds chirping and watching
as the wind blew through the leaves of the trees. They
wheeled me around the grounds so I could see rest of
the hospital. It was huge. My head swiveled from side
to side taking in every inch of the hospital grounds. I
didn't want to miss a thing. Being outside is another of
many things I will never again take for granted.

In those days before I went to rehab, my brother Brian asked me if I remembered anything from my time in the coma. I told him that I hadn't been able to hear anyone outside my head, but that I'd had fantastic dreams. I told him about some of them. Since that time, I've also told other people about my amazing dreams.

Someone brought up an interesting point about my dreams. The common thread was, yes, that I had been shot, but that I then moved forward with my life doing other things. I think my brain was already sending a positive message to the rest of my body. We were going to recover. We would get better. We would move on.

One of the dreams I told my brother about concerned my alma mater, the University of Illinois. In this dream, I had been shot, but had made a full recovery. Then, in this dream, I received a letter in the mail from Ron Zook, the head football coach. The letter stated that he had decided to give me the come-back award for players and former players at the U of I who had overcome amazing odds to achieve a goal. I was excited but confused. I never played football at Illinois. In my dream, however, I asked my brother if I had played football at the U of I, and he told me that I had been a punter there. He had gone into his room and pulled out a picture of me in my football uniform and told me that I'd only played one year, my senior year, when the starting punter went down with an injury. I had no recollection of this, but I agreed to go to the award ceremony anyway, and Ron Zook presented me with the award. I felt great. Here I was, receiving an award for coming back after being shot and hearing such kind words about my resolve and courage. This dream felt so real when I woke up, but telling it now seems silly because in waking life I never played football in college.

Another dream involved my being the emcee for a fundraising event for Vice-President Joe Biden. In this dream, I felt like it was my big shot to really break out in the speaking world. It was going to be a big feather in my cap. But on the morning of the event, I was shot in the left side of my stomach. The dream didn't tell me why I was shot, just that I was shot. I put a bandage over the wound, got dressed in my tuxedo, and went to the event. The organizers were aghast. They asked me if it was a good idea for me to do this, given that I had just been shot. I told them I'd be fine and then I went to the microphone to start the event. About half-way through the dream event, however, the pain became unbearable and I looked down to see blood seeping through the bandages. I felt sick. Then in my dream I vomited all over the lectern. I apologized and walked off the stage and went to the hospital.

Weird dream? Yes. But the really funny part is that I am actually a Republican, so the idea that I would ever be an emcee at an event for a Democratic nominee is actually a bit humorous.

As I said before, these two dreams, and all my other dreams, had the common theme of my having been shot and then moving forward to do big things with my life. My brain was clearly sending this positive message. But where did all this positivity come from?

For starters, I had some excellent role models for recovery. My grandmother (now deceased) was one of the most independent women I ever met. At eighty-three years old, she was the one who picked up all of her lady friends and drove them to church or to a restaurant. She was also the secretary for her local chapter of the American Association of Retired Persons (AARP). She was sharp as could be, and she lived by herself independently.

At least, she did so until she had a major stroke. The whole left side of her brain and body were affected, and it changed her life for her final years. All of a sudden, my grandmother, who was a former bookkeeper, could not even tell you how many coins were needed to make change for a dollar. She had trouble remembering simple things and performing simple tasks. She had to come live with us in our home for a while, but eventually she was able to move back to her own home with a live-in helper. She never lost her spirit and her resolve to try to get better. Even with her brain functioning below its normal capacity, she kept trying to improve her condition. I had never seen someone fight so hard and never give up.

My mother was also a perfect role model, as she had gone through a recovery very similar to mine. In 1999, she suffered a severe heart attack and was rushed to the nearest hospital in Chicago. But that hospital didn't have a cardiac unit, and they wouldn't release her once she got there. It took three days for her physician to assume responsibility and transport her to a hospital in the suburbs. After much discussion, the surgeons finally agreed to operate, although they believed she would die on the operating table. Not only did they save her, but they were also able to save one third of her heart. I remember walking in to see my mother when she was recovering in the hospital. It was an awful sight.

It took her months, but she eventually learned how to sit up, how to move, how to walk, and even how to dance again. She never lost her will to fight or her positive attitude to get better. At one point when she was lying in her hospital bed, she asked the doctors how long it would be until she was dancing again. The doctors told her it was unlikely she would dance again. But she responded, "I *will* dance again." It's this attitude that led her to full recovery. She helped me at every step during my recovery, in part because she'd gone through almost the exact same recovery.

In addition, my father knew how to deal with recovery because he had helped my mother through her recovery. He walked her around the shopping malls for practice just like he did with me up and down my hospital hallways. Whenever I felt like giving up, I would think about what my mom went through and how normal she is today. It kept me positive and moving in the right direction.

If the role models from my past weren't doing it for me, all I had to do was to look into the smile of Alfredo Bless when he came to visit me. His story is also amazing. After getting shot, he had to learn to deal with the new reality that he would not be able to walk again. And he rolled in every day filled with optimism. He told me that we would be shooting baskets together some day. He also talked about all the advancements in technology that help paraplegics walk again. Even now,

Alfredo is always moving forward and celebrating every small victory.

I always have lived my life with a positive attitude, but one thing I learned from my role models and from my own experience is that there really is no other choice. You have to have a positive attitude. Even if you have to dig deep to find a small victory to celebrate, you must do it.

During those moments when you feel weakest, you need to pray for strength and trust in God. To succeed in anything in life—and especially while surviving a tragedy—you need to remain hopeful and optimistic. You have no other choice. When the positive energy comes back, you have increased resolve to try and do anything. God is ready to give you that positive energy. You need to be ready to receive it.

Chapter Twelve:

The Will to Walk

Five weeks after I woke up, it was time for me to be transferred to a rehabilitation facility. I was able to sit up by now and go out in a wheelchair with help from a therapist, but I still couldn't stand up or even roll over in bed. On April 2, 2010, Good Friday, I was taken by a medical ambulance from St. Mary's Hospital in West Palm Beach to Mt. Sinai Rehabilitation Center in Miami Beach. As I was being rolled out of St. Mary's in the wheelchair, the whole ICU team of nurses, doctors, and other staff gathered to hug me and my family and say goodbye. It seemed like an episode of *ER*, a wonderful moment, but once I was in the ambulance, my mind was already racing ahead with new thoughts.

To be honest, I was scared. You'd think I would be excited about taking this next step in my recovery, that I was eager to walk again. The reality was that I was uncertain about what I would be able to do. Up to this point, I was having only moderate success just sitting up and moving my arms.

What if I couldn't walk? What if I never walked again? What if my inflexibility kept me from being able to dress myself? What if my wrists never woke up? What if I had to be dependent on other people for the rest of my life?

In the hospital, all I had to do was just lie there. Very little was expected of me. In the rehab facility, however, I would be expected to work hard. I would see the first signs of whether or not I would be able to do certain activities.

I had so many questions for the physical therapists, neurologists, and occupational therapists that came into my new room to see me. I tried to put on a smile and show a positive attitude, but inside I was petrified.

What was the potential outcome of my rehabilitation?

The initial comments from everyone at the rehab facility were positive. The neurologists told me that I had a radial nerve palsy, also known as wrist drop, in both wrists. They said it was common in situations like mine and that the nerves should repair themselves over time. My wrists would still be floppy for a while, he said, and not work well, but they should recover fully. This process, they added, could take three months to a year, but they seemed positive about the prognosis.

The therapists were even more optimistic. They told me that I would be walking in two or three weeks and that I would probably be in rehab for a total of three or four weeks.

I was skeptical. I looked up at them and said, "You are aware that I cannot stand up or even roll over in bed on my own, right?"

"We'll work hard with you," they said. "But it's up to you to make the rehab go faster. Your effort would determine the pace of your recovery."

The first thing they did was take me to a hand/wrist specialist to see what could be done about my wrists. Even when I wore a stiff brace, my wrists were so weak my fingers couldn't function. Without active wrists and fingers, my hands wouldn't be useful during the rehab process. They wheeled me down to see the specialist, a young Asian woman named Hoang.

Hoang tried all different kinds of braces on me and used various electrical stimulation treatments to the nerves of my forearm to stimulate nerve growth. But her greatest contribution to my rehab was a *Star Wars*-like contraption that she made for my right wrist, which had zero movement at the time. The device, which used pulleys and rubber bands fixed to a plastic base around my forearm, allowed me to move my fingers a bit and actually grab things. Since it was on my right wrist and I am right-handed, this was helpful for eating, drinking, and doing my occupational therapy.

A week into my rehab, my new and improved wrists and I were ready to deal with occupational therapy. This consisted of learning how to do what we do every day, from writing to brushing our teeth to putting on our socks. This work tested the limits of my patience and often left me completely frustrated. Imagine being barely flexible, having little strength, and trying to use hands and wrists that don't work well to put on and button an ordinary shirt. Even when I was putting on a T-shirt, I would spend at least fifteen minutes twisting and pulling and reaching, just to get my head and arms through the proper holes, and I rarely had the dexterity (or the strength) to pull the shirt down all the way to my waist. But I was happy just to get my head through the right hole. Some days I gave up in frustration and asked someone to dress me, but I hated that feeling. I hated feeling helpless.

I wasn't much better at the other activities of daily living. Brushing my teeth and washing my face were both difficult because I lacked the balance to stand over the sink, even if I wasn't trying to do anything else. I quickly learned to make adjustments. For instance, I soon learned that I could use each hand to brush the opposite side of my mouth. I discovered that if I had a wet wash cloth and held opposite ends of it, I could use a sawing motion to wipe off my face and chest.

Each day was amazing as I watched how my brain invented new little tricks to overcome the difficulties I was having with the easiest tasks. They took me in a wheelchair into an occupational rehab room every day. Here they did repetitive motion tasks with me that helped my muscles relearn how to do simple tasks. But it made me crazy. Two examples stand out, the boxes of nuts and bolts and the dreaded clothespin game.

For the nuts and bolts challenge, the therapist brought out a box of 100 nuts and 100 screws. Then the therapist told me to screw a nut on each screw. I could barely pick up those tiny little one-inch nuts. They seemed to be as thick as a penny. When I finally got one between my fingers, it was hard to keep from shaking as I tried to align it with the end of the screw. After half an hour, when I finally got a nut on each screw, I gave the therapist a big, satisfied smile.

"Okay," this sadist said, "now take off each of the nuts from the screws." It was maddening.

Another simple task that was incredibly difficult at the time was to fasten about twenty-five clothespins on a vertical wooden board standing in front of me on the table. The therapist told me to use only one hand to fasten all the clothespins on the board. It was nearly impossible for me to squeeze the clothespins enough to open them so I could put them on the board. Besides that, I had to reach as high as I could to get to the top of the board. When I finally got the last clothespin in place, the therapist said, "OK, now use the same hand to remove them all and put them back in the box." Another exercise in sadism. And then I had to use my other hand and do the whole thing over again. It not only stretched my physical capabilities, but it was also mentally exhausting. I knew I had to get my motor skills back. But it was really hard to concentrate on some days, especially if I was grieving on that day.

All of these fine muscle activities were difficult to relearn, but two of the most emotionally draining activities were learning to write and tie my shoes again. I could rationalize my inability to do the other tasks because of my lack of strength or flexibility, but I'd been tying my shoes and writing since I was a little boy. How hard could it be to master these simple skills again? Sometimes I tried to walk myself through the steps of tying my shoelaces, and I would get it really close. But sometimes I did it wrong. And sometimes I struggled and struggled just to get one lace around the other, and just when I was ready to give up, the shoe laces would magically end up tied. I think I might have had a little help from above on those occasions.

Learning how to write again was just plain depressing. First, I didn't know how to hold the pencil in my hand. Then, when I was able to grip the pencil, my wrists would be flopping around so much I couldn't keep it straight. That's when the therapist put the stiff braces on my wrists. We figured that would help. I confidently picked up the pencil, aimed the point at the paper… and scribbled the worst looking P I've ever seen. I knew what I wanted to do. My hand just wasn't cooperating. I couldn't draw the straight line, not to mention the curved line. I probably drew a better P when I was in kindergarten. When the therapist told me to continue with the rest of my name, I looked at her like she was crazy. Could she see that awful P I'd just drawn? That didn't matter. I had to keep trying.

The next letter looked a little bit like an A, but the T was a disaster. I couldn't get the two lines to meet and cross in a perpendicular manner. "Are you kidding me?" I asked. Then I started to cry in frustration. What kind of lawyer could I be if I could never write again? The therapist kept assuring me that I just needed practice, but it was disheartening to see that my writing skills were lower than kindergarten level. I didn't want her to see me crying, so I wiped my tears away and kept on printing, one slow letter at a time.

After three weeks, I was able to print a full sentence that was marginally legible. Cursive writing came next.

Yes, writing was going to require practice and time. I knew that time would not be an issue because I had a lot of that after I left the hospital. I just had to make sure that I kept my resolve to keep practicing writing letters and concentrating on making straight lines. I am sure this sounds boring and simplistic. Maybe it was, but I had to keep on moving forward. That meant constant practice. Eventually, I succeeded, and, of course, I celebrated.

Learning to walk was another challenging and humbling experience. First of all, you have to imagine how difficult it was for me in the beginning to simply sit up in bed. My body had been horizontal for four months. It was not used to fighting against gravity. This included my heart's ability to pump blood and oxygen down to my feet and up through my upper torso into my head.

To help me get ready to start to walk, they gave me these long, white stockings that were extra tight. I wore them to help with my circulation. After every other activity that needed my attention, focus, and resolve, I usually had little fuel left in the tank when it came time to practicing walking. I had to dig deep to find the strength for this task. Actually, I was scared.

Each day, the physical therapist bounced in, brimming with excitement and anticipation. He always asked me if I was ready to work that day, then he started motivating me. Once my head was in it, he lifted me up and put me in the wheelchair. Then, walking ahead of me, he made me use my feet to power my way down the hallway to the therapy room. That was hard work. Sometimes I was exhausted before we even began therapy, but I knew that everything we were doing was to help me get better.

After I wheeled myself into the therapy room, another therapist came to assist. As I sat in my wheelchair and stared up at them, the two therapists put the walker in front of me. We counted to three. Then, in one quick motion, the therapist behind me helped to lift me into a standing position. My legs wobbling, I tried to balance myself and gripped the walker with all my might. I wanted to keep my legs from shaking.

Therapist: "Take a step, buddy."

Me: "I'm trying, but my leg won't do it. What do I do?"

Therapist: "Just try to move it forward a little bit."

After a struggle that could have lasted several minutes, I slid my left foot forward. And then I slid my right one forward. After I took four of these sliding steps, I plopped back down in the wheelchair, thoroughly exhausted. We tried it again, one step, two steps, three steps, four steps. After that, we did stretching and leg-strengthening exercises. I knew from the start that this was going to be a long grueling process, but as the days went by, the therapists kept telling me to pick up my feet when I walked. They also reminded me that I am not a little old man who has to shuffle his feet. One of them stood behind me and instructed me to put my heel down first, then my toe. But this was a concept I just couldn't get. My feet were not cooperating. I walked like Frankenstein's monster, with stiff legs, stomping around the room. Finally, they had me stand against the wall for half an hour, hitting my heel against the floor, lifting it up, and hitting it against the floor again. That's how I learned to walk again, heel-toe.

I began to see progress every few days. It was usually measured in distance. First it was four steps. Soon it was nine steps. Then we were measuring by feet. I could walk twenty feet, then forty feet, then a hundred feet. I was still using a walker for support, but after lying in a bed for four months, it felt good to be able to walk even a short distance. All of the other therapists were also supportive. They all knew my story, and they applauded and cheered every time I came shuffling along where they were working with other patients.

One day during my final week of rehabilitation, they wheeled me up to the parallel bars to practice walking. You've seen this routine on TV. The idea is that you hold on to the parallel bars, one on each side of you, rather than the walker in front of you, and you take steps. On this day, Adam, the therapist, asked me if I wanted to try taking a step without holding the bars. I told him that I didn't think I was ready. I was scared. He gently encouraged me to give it a try anyway.

We counted to three and I stood up. I grabbed the bars for balance and to steady my wobbling legs. As soon as I regained my balance—and my composure—I let go of the bar. I stood there for a second, just waiting to see what would happen. Nothing bad happened.

I took one step forward, then another, and then another. I was walking all by myself! Adam was following me closely with the wheelchair in case I needed to sit down, but after taking six steps, I told him to take the chair back to the starting point. Then I turned around and took six steps back to the wheelchair and then sat down in it.

The minute I sat down in the chair, I felt it coming. An outpouring of feelings that had been bottled up inside me started to gush out. I started crying like a baby. But I was now a toddler! I was happy and so relieved. It was such a tremendous victory for me to take my first independent steps.

Every therapist in the room was standing there, open-mouthed. Then they started to clap for me. They were excited, even though I just kept sitting there crying. The spectrum of emotions during these first two months was wide and varied, but at this moment, it was pure elation.

As I learned to walk at the rehabilitation facility, the therapists began to prepare me to go home. On, April 19, 2010, in the final week, they told me on that I would be going home on Saturday. That made me excited and nervous at the same time. Would I be able to live on my own? I knew it would not be an easy task, but I also knew that my parents would be there to help me. I also knew I had the resolve to keep moving forward. I was ready for the next challenge. Nothing was going to hold me back.

There was just one problem. It dawned on me as I started to think about going home. I was only five days away from going home, and I still didn't have the flexibility or dexterity to wipe my own bottom after using the bathroom. I was getting really nervous about this because, while I had no problem with calling a nurse to wipe me, I was not going to have my mother wipe me. I was thirty-seven years old. I was not going to let that happen.

So I began a stretching program. Each day, I stretched and moved and tried different ways to get the job done. Nothing was working well, and each day's failure built more pressure in me. I could feel myself getting closer, but I still couldn't do it completely. On Thursday night, I was really getting worried. We were only two days away from going home and I still didn't have it down. I went to bed and prayed for strength. I prayed for flexibility. I prayed to be spared the humiliation of calling my mother.

And on Friday afternoon, when my parents arrived, I was bustling with excitement. I kept peering around the corner to see them coming toward my room. I couldn't wait to share my news with them. A miracle had happened over night. As my parents walked into my room, and before they could say a word, I proclaimed my good news.

"I wiped my butt today!"

Chapter Thirteen:

Back to Life. The Daily Battle

On April 23, 2010, as I finished my final week at Mt. Sinai Rehabilitation Center, I was still feeling apprehensive about going home and having to face the real world. It may sound crazy, but I had started to get comfortable in the hospital. Meals came at a set time, visitation always occurred between certain hours, rehab exercises were on a schedule, and the rest of the time I just slept or watched television.

Going home meant that I would have to face my fears, deal with new challenges, and truly begin living in my new reality in the real world. First, I was still worried about walking back into my condo for the first time and knowing Lisa would not be there. Other sources of worry? I knew I still couldn't walk very well, and I had trouble even envisioning how I would make it from the car all the way into my condo. Showering was going to be difficult, too, as I still could not stand for very long, and using the toilet was an experience in and of itself. I worried about dressing myself. I worried about cooking for myself, setting the table, cleaning up afterward. I worried about cleaning my house. As focused as I was on moving forward, I felt very anxious about leaving the hospital.

One person that helped me stay focused was a neuropsychologist at Mt. Sinai Rehab named Dr. Lynn Schram. Most people who came in to speak with me—psychologists, priests, and physicians—made me angry or withdrawn. The other psychologists and the priests had come in to try and make me feel better, and they all used their own techniques. And they all went down in flames. I was not ready to be told to feel better. I was always defensive and ready to debate these people.

Dr. Schram didn't try to "help me understand" why this happened, and he didn't try to make me "feel better." He had no interest in debating me. Instead, he listened to me. He quietly listened to my concerns, and then we talked about ways I could overcome my fears and apprehension. Instead of advice, he gave me a tool that helped me immensely when I went back to my condo. We did a visualization exercise in the rehab hospital that I would find myself using over and over during the next six months as I navigated difficult situations. Basically, he asked me to visualize what my first day was going to be like, from the time I got out of the car until I went to sleep that night in my own bed.

Dr. Schram: "When you open the door to your condo, what do you see?"

Me: "Well, on the left side of the entrance, there is a framed world map stuck with push pins for all the places that I have traveled."

Dr. Schram: "As you take a few steps inside, what do you see?"

Me: "The kitchen is on the left. I'll be looking into the living room. I will also see the view of the bay from my balcony. It's gorgeous."

Dr. Schram: "Describe that view for me."

Me: "I'm on the thirtieth floor. There's a park below, with tennis courts, a dog park, and basketball and volleyball courts. To the right of the park, there's Biscayne Bay, and from my balcony you can see all the way across the bay to Sunny Isles."

Dr. Schram: "What will you do once you enter your condo and go past the entrance?"

Me: "Probably, I'll just walk over to the couch, sit down, and decompress so I can take everything in. It might be too emotional. Then I'll probably have my mom get me a glass of water from the kitchen."

Dr. Schram: "When you're sitting on the couch, what are you thinking about?"

Me: "I'll probably just be taking in my surroundings and looking at my pictures on the shelves. The White Sox brick I have from the old Comiskey Park. The JCI awards sitting in the entertainment center."

The visualization went on like this until we had gone through my entire first day home. He had me visualize not only what I would see, but how I would feel and what I would be thinking about. It was an interesting exercise that I had in fact used in many of my training seminars, but I had no idea how effective it would be for me the next day when I entered my condo for the first time.

Since I could walk only about 300 feet at a time, my main focus when I left the rehab facility was simply to walk all the way to the elevator and then walk out to my dad's car. Dad had pulled the car up to the front entrance, so I didn't have to walk too far, but when I got to the car and climbed into the back seat, I had used up all my energy.

Getting into a car had been another one of my therapy exercises. We had used a little makeshift car in the therapy room. I knew what to expect, and it was difficult, but after falling into the back seat of the real car, I managed to pull my legs into the car. It was so weird to be outside a hospital, to be in a car. I was very anxious as we pulled away from the rehab facility and started heading home.

My condo was only ten minutes away, and as we crossed Biscayne Bay, I used that time to prepare myself. We then pulled up to the front door of my building. I pulled myself out of the car, using the door frame. My legs were shaking. I steadied myself and looked around. The doorman and other front desk people were there, and they looked overjoyed to see me. It was a warm and encouraging homecoming.

My next giant step was to go up in the elevator and then go into my condo. My parents opened the door and walked in ahead of me. I thought I would be frozen, but I just stepped right in and looked to my right and left. There was the world map with the push pins still in it. There was my kitchen. My living room. I took a few more steps. I walked past the kitchen and into the living room and to my sliding glass door. I looked down at the park below and the beautiful bay on my right.

By that time, I was at my limit for steps. I needed to sit down, so I walked to the couch. After sitting down, I took a deep breath and looked straight ahead. There was my entertainment center with the TV, the White Sox brick from Comiskey Park, and the JCI awards. Everything was just as I'd described to Dr. Schram. I couldn't believe how effective that visualization exercise was.

During that entire first day, I never broke down and cried, not even once. The rest of the day also went just as I had described it to Dr. Schram. That made it a lot easier on my psychological state. My mother brought me a drink, and then my father and I made a schedule for me to practice walking. I turned on the television and just stared at it for an hour. I was doing okay! It seemed a little funny, but I knew right then that I was going to be able to do this. Silently, inside my head, I celebrated.

After two hours, my father broke the silence and told me it was time to practice walking. I was hesitant to stand up again because it was difficult and painful to even try, but he insisted. He had suggested an option, that I could decide how often I wanted to practice walking, and I had agreed to do it for ten minutes every two hours. He didn't nag me or make me feel guilty. He just reminded me of my agreement. He also said he knew I had the strength to do this and get better.

The next thing I had to do, however, was put on my shoes back on and tie the laces. This was a ten-minute process in itself. My parents sat close by, watching me and even offering to help, but I waved them off because I needed to learn to do these things by myself. Once I had my shoes on, I had to struggle to get off the couch.

Getting up is another thing I will never take for granted again. I tried to slide forward on the couch and then roll to my right to get some leverage on the armrest. Then I had to push myself up and try to get my legs under me. One final push off the armrest, and I was upright, trying to regain my balance. By the time we were ready to walk out the door, fifteen minutes had passed, and all I'd done was put on my shoes and stand up. It was going to be slow.

For the first week, I only had enough strength and energy to walk up and down the hallway on my floor. I walked slowly, with my dad walking to my left and holding my elbow in case I lost my balance. It took about fifteen minutes to walk up and down my hall, one tiny step at a time, but soon I was enjoying our stroll. My dad and I talked about how I was feeling and discussed what we had read in the paper that day. It was nice to just spend some time with my dad, even in these extreme circumstances.

My recovery was not all positive, of course. I had to battle severe depression every morning. I would wake up each day and look to my right and see that Lisa was not there. I was sleeping on my side of the bed and leaving her side made, so each day when I woke up, it was painfully obvious that she was gone and never coming back. This was an instant reminder that I would never see her again, that I was going to have to go through this whole recovery without her. She would have made it so much easier, and I know she would have been my biggest cheerleader. Yes, it was really hard to look at the empty side of the bed.

The next thing that happened every morning was that when I moved my arms under my pillow, my wrists still flopped around. They weren't working yet, and that made it difficult to do anything, from flipping over my pillow to pulling the sheet up closer to my face.

When I finally tried to sit up in bed, my whole neurovascular system was out of whack, and I typically got so dizzy that I had to lie back down for a few minutes. After two or three tries, I was able to sit up and push my legs over the side of the bed.

My whole body was incredibly sore at this time because the muscles were regrowing at an accelerated pace. Imagine the worst pain you felt after you went to the gym for the first time after a long hiatus. Now multiply that discomfort by ten. The pain I felt in my legs and arms was excruciating. I had a five-minute struggle to get my feet on the floor, then I had to roll over to use my arms to push myself off of the bed so I could stand up. This was worse than the couch because there was no armrest to push off from. I had to give myself a really strong shove to get upright. Once I was standing (and balanced), I had to walk the fifteen feet to the bathroom. This was no easy task, and with each shuffling step, the pain seared through my legs. I was walking like I was holding an apple between my thighs. By the time I made it to the bathroom, I was nearly defeated.

It was a half hour process to open my eyes and get as far as the bathroom. That hard work took its toll. I could feel the despair and frustration deep inside my stomach, and it worked its way up to my head. If I hadn't begun to cry up until this point, the next moment would put me over the top.

As I stood before the bathroom mirror, looking at my weak and frail body, I knew the next step was to remove the bandages from my stomach so I could take a shower. Sometimes I stood there for ten minutes. I didn't want to see what was under the bandages. I had been left with huge scars all over my torso from the numerous surgeries when they opened up my chest cavity and rib cage. There were also numerous small scars from the tubes, and I have two major scars that may require some future surgery at some point. One scar is over twelve inches long and three inches across. Another scar is only six inches long, but goes much deeper into my torso. Once the bandages came off, I could barely look at the person staring back at me in the mirror.

I would almost crawl into the shower and sit on my little shower chair as I tried to flop my wrist up to the soap dish and grab the soap. I felt defeated and humiliated. My brain moved back and forth among all the trials that were putting me in this depressed mental state. There was nothing I could do about it, but it was just hard for me to spend the first hour of every day battling these terrible demons.

After my shower, I got dressed. That was another thirty-minute process as I pulled the shirt over my head and struggled to pull it down. Putting on socks and pants took incredible patience. I then walked into the kitchen and made breakfast, a bowl of cereal. It took two hands to pour milk due to my limp wrists and if it was a full carton of milk, I would nearly drop it while pouring. My parents, who were staying with me, were there in the kitchen and living room, but they were understanding enough to give me my space and let me deal with these issues. Within three minutes of eating my cereal, I usually just broke down, hunched over and sobbing into my bowl. I actually watched my tears roll off my nose and drip into the milk. How pathetic! How humbling! But I knew it was a process that I had to go through if I wanted to keep moving forward.

After breakfast, I joined my dad on the couch to read the paper. Every two hours, he reminded me that it was time to practice walking, so we went through that whole routine again. When I had free time, I practiced writing. If I felt really adventurous, I tried to make myself a meal. My mother always offered to help me, but I was determined to learn to do things on my own again. Even with the constant focus on getting better and relearning the activities of daily living, I still cried two to three times per day.

But don't get me wrong. This wasn't a pity-party anymore, and I wasn't alone. It was merely a part of the grieving process. There was tremendous support for me during these first several weeks at home. Not only did I have my parents and my brothers, but I also had a steady stream of friends, coworkers, and acquaintances who dropped by to see me and make sure I was doing well. There were, in fact, so many people trying to come to my condo to see me that I had to make a schedule.

I truly believe that the love and support that I received from my family and friends made all the difference. To this day, I am grateful for that support.

Even with that support, however, I knew it was up to me to get out of bed each day. I had to have enough self-motivation to make this happen.

As I made it through each day, I developed a three-pronged strategy for my total recovery: (1) Focus on me getting better. (2) Pray for strength. (3) Become my own cheerleader. Instead of focusing on all the things that were depressing each morning, I went back to celebrating every small victory. If the situation was difficult, I prayed for enough strength to make it through one more day. Finally, when I felt like giving up, I encouraged myself and talked to myself. I was motivating myself to keep on going. This was now my approach to life.

Chapter Fourteen:

Appreciating Every Aspect of Life

In those first five months, I continued to use the techniques I had used in the hospital. I also made sure that I followed the lessons I was learning. Most importantly, I concentrated on the positive things in my life and avoided pity-parties at all costs. I celebrated every victory, no matter how small or large, and watched for any sign of improvement in any area of my physical or mental state. My focus was always on moving forward and tackling the next challenge.

The interesting thing about my new positive attitude was that it really wasn't new at all. I have been a positive person all my life. Generally, prior to the shooting, I had appreciated all of the little things in life and every morning when I woke up, I always felt incredible. I was ready to take on the world.

I even taught seminars and gave speeches about positive leadership and expecting good things to happen to you in your career and life. There are things you can do in your life to help improve your positive outlook. I already knew these things, of course, and I firmly believe that this positive attitude helped me get through this tragedy. I naturally look for the silver-lining in any situation.

People often ask me now if I have a new appreciation for life. I think they want to hear me say that my whole view of the world has been changed, that I have a new sense of purpose. Sometimes I think they want to hear me say that I had a major transformation, as if my life came out of *It's a Wonderful Life*. Truth be told, there was no major transformation, just a strong and painful reminder to have a positive mindset and move forward. As I was in recovery, I just needed to go back to the way I always approached life.

If this sounds a bit too pragmatic, let me tell you that the experience was indeed very emotional. I was grief-stricken for many months, and as I said earlier, my morning routine usually ended with tears spilling into my cereal.

I struggled with thoughts about God. Why had the tragedy happened? Why had it happened to me? I came to appreciate certain little things that I used to take for granted, like getting out of a chair with ease. But was there a major breakthrough transformation for me? No, not really.

This is not to say that other people do not experience major, life-altering transformations. I am sure that as a result of a life-altering event, some people develop a new purpose in life, become less selfish and more giving, or take their lives in an entirely new direction. This is a completely acceptable course of action. But so is what happened to me.

I don't think anyone can feel unfulfilled if a major life tragedy or catastrophe does not produce some sort of Zen-like enlightenment. It might, but it might not. In part, it depends on your outlook on life before the tragedy. As long as you are positive and keep moving forward, you will make it.

That being said, I am doing something with the second chance that God gave me, and that is to help others overcome tragedy and appreciate their own lives. Although my outlook did not change dramatically, I think I might be able to assist others with their outlook. People are unique and react to situations differently. My goal is to help people refocus how they view their recovery while placing their trust in God.

I still have the same overall appreciation of life that I had before the incident. The difference now is the magnitude of the things that I appreciate. I celebrate every small victory as much as I celebrate a job promotion. For example, when I get up out of a chair or stand up after lying on the floor, it's a really big deal. Every time I do that now, I get a little smile and a feeling of accomplishment.

For many months, I couldn't do either of these tasks very well. If I were on the floor for some reason, I had to roll over to my knees, crawl over to a chair, grab the seat of the chair, and pull myself up half way before pushing off to a standing position. Sounds like a lot of work, right? It was. But that struggle to stand up gave me a new appreciation for how simple it is to do it now, two years later.

I remember one time, about six months after I woke up, when I was playing with a friend's dog on the floor.

When my friend said it was time to go, I put my hands on the floor, tucked my feet under my body, and stood straight up…just like a normal, uninjured person! I had a huge grin on my face and was beaming with my accomplishment. My friend asked me what I was so happy about.

"I couldn't do that last week," I said. It was such a simple task and such a small moment in my life, but I was truly grateful that God had given me the strength to do such a simple thing as stand up.

Another example is any action that involves my wrists. My left wrist started to wake up about eight months after I woke up, but my right wrist took more than a year to wake up fully. In the beginning, I couldn't do something as basic as use a scissors because I couldn't lift my thumb to open and close the blades. Initially, I bought a scissors that opens automatically. Yes, they do have those, mostly for people with arthritis. But the first time I was able to use a real scissors, I felt fantastic. To this day, every time I pull out a pair of scissors, I marvel at my ability to use such a simple tool.

I went back to work three weeks after I left the rehabilitation center. About a month after that, I started going to the courthouse again for hearings and trials. During those appointments, I had to wear a tie. Now, tying a tie is not the easiest thing in the world to master even if your wrists are working properly. When your wrists flop around and have little strength, it becomes nearly impossible. Day after day, I tried, with no success, but I kept trying because I kept getting closer and closer to getting that knot right. One day, when I finally pulled the tie into place perfectly, I just stood there, staring into the mirror and smiling. For the rest of that day, I walked around my condo building, my office, and the courthouse telling everyone that I had tied my own tie that day. I didn't care how silly it sounded. I was celebrating another significant victory

I became very accustomed to trying things over and over again until I succeeded. I often had to adapt my approach or try some new approach altogether. Typing on my computer is a perfect example. Prior to the incident, I was a very fast typist, and I used to type many of my own letters and memoranda at work. After the incident, while I was still wearing my wrist braces, I had to learn how to "hunt and peck" with one finger on each hand. As my wrists were waking up, I managed to do this faster and faster.

Then one day, my secretary walked in to my office, looked at me, and began laughing. Pointing at my keyboard, she asked me what I was doing. I looked down. I was naturally typing with my left hand (my left wrist had woken up) while using the one-finger approach with my right hand. Not only that, but I was typing very quickly using this method.

I hadn't noticed. I have no idea when it started, but it just showed me that my body could adapt to any situation as long as I kept trying to do things. As I sit here today, typing the manuscript for this book, I realize that I type completely normally now and at the same speed as before the incident. You have to start somewhere. During this trial and error process of learning the activities of daily life, I also discovered that it is essential to keep my sense of humor. This was especially true when I wasn't able to do simple tasks. Failure often produced humorous results. One perfect anecdote shows how funny it was when I tried to get dressed in the morning. It was incredibly difficult for me to pull a polo or T-shirt over my head because my wrists didn't work, and I also had very little flexibility to pull the shirt down. Until you are in my situation, you cannot imagine how difficult it can be to put the shirt on. While my parents were still living with me during those first few weeks at home, I often came out in my underwear with my arms stuck over my head wrapped up in a shirt that I couldn't pull down. My face was lost in the shirt as I wandered out into the living room asking for someone to help me pull it down.

One day, my mother told me that César, the doorman downstairs, had told her that he would help me if I ever needed anything or got stuck. I started laughing. "Mom," I said, "imagine me getting off the elevator, walking into the lobby in my underwear, with my arms stuck over my head and wrapped up in my shirt." We all had a good laugh.

Every little task was so hard in the beginning that when I learned to do it again, it felt as big as running a marathon. For example, when I had to button a dress shirt, I had to allow half an hour. Each button was a difficult task that could take three to five minutes. I would try to grasp the button with my finger, but my wrists were not strong enough to help me get it through the little hole. Sometimes, I would walk into the lobby and ask the front desk people to finish buttoning my shirt or my sleeves. I was just happy when I got most of them buttoned.

BLESSED TO SURVIVE

There were big victories to celebrate, too. The first trial I had about four and a half months after I woke up ended with a nice victory. In that same week, I gave my first speech to the Dania Chamber of Commerce. These two victories made me feel like my old self. Plus, I now had an inspirational story to tell.

I presented my first JCI seminar on July 18, 2010, one week after those two events and it felt like nothing had changed (other than the fact that it was more difficult for me to write on a flip chart). The big thing for me was that recognition that the big victories seemed no more important than any of the small victories described above. This recognition was a pivotal point in my recovery. Now I knew I could find happiness in the most insignificant moments in my life.

As I began to give speeches about my incident, I took greater ownership of my recovery. First, I was asked by a church near Detroit to share my story. I was a little nervous about whether I would be able to make it all the way through the speech without breaking down. What did I do? I prayed for strength and God was all too happy to deliver it.

During that speech at St. Joseph's Church in Lake Orion, Michigan, I only had three times where I started to get emotional. But they didn't throw me off topic, and I felt God's strength inside me as I shared my message. I met many amazing people that day, and there were several people in the audience that really seemed to relate to the message. I felt good sharing my story and helping others in the process.

My next speech was going to be a big one. This

was the presentation in Osaka, Japan, at the JCI World Congress, the event that I had booked before the shooting and which was the catalyst for my quick recovery. Every time I did not want to practice walking, I thought about my speech in Japan. That gave me the motivation to stand up and walk. Even before I left the hospital, I daydreamed about what it would be like to walk on stage at the JCI World Congress. This is the main JCI event. It draws more than 8,000 JCI members from around the world. Within days of leaving the hospital, I sent out an email message to several thousand JCI members who had put up a web page of support for me. I told them emphatically that I would be in Osaka to speak.

As the conference date grew closer, I was excited, but also very nervous. I knew the outpouring of love and support would be enormous, but I wondered if it would be too overwhelming. Again, I worried about whether I would get overemotional on stage. I wasn't sure I would be able to share my story in the fifteen minutes I was given to speak about the tragedy before I turned to the real topic that I was there to speak about. After all, the speech in Michigan had gone on for nearly an hour.

I went to Japan. The morning of the speech, when I stepped into the assembly room, I could feel a buzz in the air. For starters, it was hard for me to walk through the room because I would get stopped every couple of feet to receive a hug from one of my JCI friends. It was a wonderful feeling to see the warmth in their eyes. They really cared about me, and I know they prayed for me, too. I don't usually get very nervous when I speak publicly, even when it's for extremely large audiences, but this time the emotions inside of me turned my legs feel to jelly. As the announcer said my name, I took my first steps out onto the stage and looked at the audience.

What did I see? A sea of people standing up and clapping. It wasn't just the polite applause that any speaker gets. No, this was more. It was an outpouring of hope and love that I had never experienced before. My eyes instantly welled up with tears as I looked out at several thousand people were standing and cheering and clapping for me.

Many of these people had prayed for me every day while I was in my coma. They were the reason I had worked so hard to make sure that I could be there with them. I felt a wave of emotion smack me in the stomach, and I had to compose myself before opening my mouth. I took a deep breath and walked to the middle of the stage, but they wouldn't stop clapping. When they finally sat down, I was able to tell my story.

As I spoke, I could see people crying. These were people who had been pulling for me for a whole year. This was the first chance most of them got to see me. I told my story, and with each word, I felt a stronger connection to the audience. I could see long-time friends there, my parents in the front row, people I had never met. When I finished, they gave me another round of passionate applause.

And I realized right then and there that I wanted to help other people and spread a message of hope for those who have experienced tragedy. Before the incident, I had spoken all over the world to audiences of thousands of people, but this was different. The reaction was different. It is one thing to give people pragmatic tips for leadership and management. It is a whole other ballgame to touch people when you speak because you share commonality, especially when that commonality is a tragic experience.

I went on to give speeches in Chicago, Miami, Cincinnati, Istanbul, and other cities. I even spoke at the largest wooden cathedral in the western hemisphere, which is located in Paramaribo, Suriname, in South America. People always came up to me afterward and shared their own stories of survival. They thanked me for giving them hope and being a good example of survival. I always responded that there is nothing special about me. All I did was ask God for strength. He's the one they should thank. (But I do appreciate hearing the kind words from all those folks.)

After everything I've been through, I can still tell you that there was no major life transformation. My outlook on life hasn't changed. If anything, my survival confirmed my prior outlook that it is always better to stay positive and look for the silver lining in any situation. At the same time, I appreciate the little things in life a whole lot more. They carry equal weight to the big victories in life. I will never take things for granted again, and I thank God for every victory he allows me to celebrate every single day.

Chapter Fifteen:

Get Off the Stool!

As I began preparing for the talks I would be giving, it dawned on me that people might have a hard time relating to someone in my situation. Either they have never been in a truly tragic place in their lives or they have trouble seeing beyond their own problems. How could I describe my situation in terms that people could relate to and understand? I wanted a simple analogy to describe my way of thinking about life and tragedy. It's easy to tell people to just be more positive and to pull themselves up by their bootstraps. It's also easy to use tough love and tell victims to suck it up and move on. I could also paint a positive picture of the future and encourage listeners to move on for the sake of their own mental health.

What I really struggled with, however, was to find a way to describe how I felt every morning for many months after I woke up from the coma. Every day, I engaged in the battle with the bed. As I stated earlier, every day started as I opened my eyes to a grim new reality that just got worse and worse until it ended with tears in my cereal.

So what made me get up every day?

Then it came to me: my life was like a boxing match. It's a series of boxing matches, a new one every morning. In boxing, you face different opponents who have varying degrees of strength and skill. For some fights, you're in perfect shape, both mentally and physically. You move about the ring with cat-like agility and your punches feel like they're packed with dynamite. You feel like Muhammad Ali—"Float like a butterfly, sting like a bee. I am the greatest!"

At times like this, your defense is impenetrable. You anticipate every punch before it comes anywhere near you. Your corner man is giving you great advice to stick and move, and he's also encouraging you to be aggressive and take the fight to your opponent. You have no fear. The fight seems effortless. You're in a zone.

But that's not true all the time. Sometimes you feel more like Rocky Balboa. You're just trying to survive until the next round. Perhaps you're unprepared or ill-prepared, you're out of shape, you're in the wrong mind-set for that fight. Or your opponent is too big, too strong, too fierce. You get punched in face over and over and over. All you're aware of is pain. Your opponent's body blows are taking away your ability to breathe normally, and after a series of combination punches to your noggin, you can't even think straight. You're repeatedly knocked down and have to scrape and claw your way back to your feet. Sometimes you have to use the ropes to pull yourself up. And then, just when you feel like you're ready to give up, the bell rings.

Back to your corner you slink. You sit down on that hard wooden stool. You try to collect thoughts, but your head is spinning. What on earth happened in that last round? You want to wish away the agony, but all you can feel is that pulsating, searing pain. So you try to assess what went wrong. Maybe you can figure out a way to prevent this bigger, faster opponent from repeatedly bashing your head in.

In a flash, you've got people standing in front of you, yelling at you. But they're all blurry. You can't concentrate of what they're saying until, finally it dawns on you—they're trying to help you. Finally you recognize your corner man and the water boy. They're trying to tend to your wounds and offer you advice and encouragement at the same time. You sit there and try to focus on their words:

Corner man: "You have to dodge that jab. Block that right hook."

As if it were that easy, you say to yourself. You look up at him and he continues giving advice.

"You have the speed," he says. "Move in, pop him, and step back."

All you can do is hold your head. *Advice and encouragement might help right now if my legs didn't feel like rubber and my head like a punching bag.*

Corner man: "Get back in there! Take the fight to him!"

Your mind stops for a second. *Why doesn't he get in there and fight this guy? Hey, man, how about helping me off this stool? Maybe if I pray to a higher power, this will all go away. Somebody help me!*

The truth is that nobody is going to help you get off that stool. Nobody is going to push you back into the fight. When the bell rings to start the next round, you can either sit there on the stool wallowing in pain or you can get back into the fight and try to turn your fortunes around. Your corner man isn't going to lift you off that stool. The water boy isn't going to pull you off that stool. It's your move.

And if you pray to God to lift you off that stool, good luck waiting for little angels to fly down and waft you up. Nope, that's not how it works. You are not a puppet with strings. There's no puppet-master to move you off that stool. God doesn't work us like marionettes. Want to get off that stool? Do it yourself. You will only think about getting off that stool because you need to do it. You will only force yourself off that stool because you want to do it.

Now before you crucify me for blasphemy, hear me out. God has a role in the fight. But he is not necessarily going to assume physical form and fight for you. In my opinion, God is in your corner. He's your strength coach. He's trained you and given you the strength you need every time you step into that ring. Because he's trained you, he knows exactly how much strength you have for the fight.

In boxing, when someone in your corner thinks you can't or shouldn't continue the fight, they throw in the towel for you so you can live to fight another day. Throwing in the towel puts an end to the fight. In your life, God is the one holding the towel. He will never give you a tougher opponent than you can face. If he sees that you can't fight anymore, he'll throw in the towel for you.

However, because he knows exactly how strong you are and how much you can take, he won't throw in the towel while he thinks you can still fight the good fight. For this reason, you should always know that you have the strength to get yourself up off that stool and back into the fight. If you didn't have the strength, if you had no more fight left in you, if you had no chance at a comeback in this fight, God would throw in the towel for you.

I know this is true. He threw in the towel for me when I couldn't take anymore. He proved it to me. It was the second week after I woke up from the three-month coma. I was lying in my hospital bed and waiting for my parents to arrive. They always came at one in the afternoon, not before, not later. They were always right on-time.

At 12:55, I always tried to turn my head as far as I could so I could watch for them. As the clock ticked closer to 1:00, I felt my excitement building. At the same time, I felt vulnerable and scared. Lying there in such pain was so new to me in those days that only the calming presence of my parents seemed to ease my suffering.

One day, the clock moved past 1:00. No parents! Then it was 1:15. Still no parents. The clock kept moving…1:30, 1:45, 2:00. Still no parents. I went into a panic. I was sure every kind of terrible thing I could think of had happened to my mom and dad. Maybe they'd been in a car accident on the I-95. Maybe my father had had a stroke from all the stress. Maybe my mother had had another heart attack. I was positive that something bad had happened, and since I was still in my pity-party mode, I let myself become more and more depressed as each minute passed. How could this happen to me? I had already lost my wife. I had just woken up from a coma and couldn't move. Why was there one more burden being added to my misery?

The truth is that my divine strength coach would never have let more happen to me. He had already thrown the towel in for me so that I could live to fight another day. Sure enough, my parents came in to my room shortly after 2:00. I was already crying, and they could see that their tardiness had upset me. What had happened? Traffic was really bad, plus they'd had some difficulties getting ready that morning.

I was just happy they were finally there, and it was at that moment that I realized God was not adding to my burdens. He knew I had little strength right then. I decided I just had to trust him. He was starting a new training program with me to give me more strength.

I have run into many little bumps in the road to recovery, but none of them were overwhelming. I trusted God to rebuild my inner-strength because he knew that I would come out as a fiercer fighter. But I needed to have time to heal and train. After hearing one of my speeches on the subject and using the boxing analogy, one pastor told me that evil had nearly knocked me out, but God had saved me. Now, he is training me harder, and evil is quaking in its boots in anticipation of the next fight. How fitting!

Just as God has given you the strength to get off your stool, he also puts people in your life to help you continue to fight. There are people he sends to your corner to give you advice and encouragement—your pastor or priest, your family, your therapist, your best friends. They'll be there to support you, they'll tend your wounds, they'll speak words of encouragement and offer you advice on how to make a comeback in the fight.

But no one will get you off that stool except for you.

In speaking with other people who have experienced tragedy and reading stories of countless other victims, I have noticed that an alarming number of people are just sitting on the stool, passively waiting for something to happen. They pray every day and wait for someone to lift them off the stool. They stare blankly at the helpers already in their corner and look for someone new to arrive and pull them off the stool. But even when their friends and family try to lift them up, they just sit there. It's as if they make themselves heavier. They won't budge.

But I have also met other people and heard other stories about people who experience a tremendous loss and hardly let their butt hit the stool before they're getting back up and into the fight. These are wonderful examples of people who trust that God has given them the strength to move forward with their lives. They welcome the corner men and the coaches God has put in their lives to give them encouragement and advice. The key is that they don't get blinded by pity-parties. Instead, they look for ways to get back into the fight as they acknowledge the blessings God is giving them. They recognize that certain people were sent into their lives to help them grow.

I eventually came to that same realization. It was no coincidence that Alfredo Bless came into my life in the hospital. God sent him to break me out of my pity-parties. There were too many signs that show Alfredo was sent to me. For starters, I was his last patient to visit as a volunteer before he changed hospitals. Second, his alias after he was shot was Patrick. Third, he had been through a shooting incident himself and could speak directly to me about the steps to recovery. Finally, in case I still didn't know who sent him, God sent someone named Bless.

And God didn't send me just one person. He put my parents and the rest of my family in my corner. He sent the hospital chaplain, Cathy Kino, plus various other pastors and priests who gave me encouragement. I had a steady stream of friendly nurses and nursing assistants who really cared about me and gave me support. Dr. Schram gave me tools to deal with difficult situations to come. My boss, my friend Arrey, and my brother Brian all gave me goals: I had to get back to my job, give the speech in Japan, enter a biking race. In fact, when you add in all of the friends and coworkers who were supporting and encouraging me, it's easy to see that my corner of the ring was crowded.

God may send various people into your life, but these people won't do it for you. He gives you the strength to move forward, but he won't do the heavy lifting for you. He's rooting for you at every stage of the fight, but he won't put on the gloves himself. He is watching over you every day. Pray to him for strength, but know that in the end, it's up to you, and only you, to get up off that stool.

Even with strength from God, you have to do it yourself.

Chapter Sixteen:

Carrying the Burden. My Medal

When bad things happen to us, they don't have to be as tragic as getting shot in the stomach by a sociopath. Your tragedy may not be as great as mine, but whatever happens, large or small, we have to deal with it. People are always asking me, "How do you move past a tragedy like this? How do you get over it?" *Move past it?* I think to myself. *Get over it? Are you serious?*

When something happens to you like what happened to me, something that nearly destroys you physically, mentally, emotionally, and spiritually, you do not "get over it" or "move past it." It's a burden you have to carry with you for the rest of your life.

Your tragedy becomes a part of who you are. It affects the makeup of your character. When people ask me how to deal with their own tragedy, I tell them to quit trying to move past it. What I tell them is that they need to learn how to carry it.

That's the beauty of this free will that God has given us. When bad things happen, yes, we have to carry the burden, but we get to choose *how* we carry it. Many people carry their burden like a giant boulder hanging around their neck. It weighs them down, and they sink deeper and deeper into depression or self-pity. These people understand that the burden cannot be overcome, but they also see it as an event that ruined their lives. They remember the lives they were leading, and the only new script for the future they can see is one that is increasingly negative. Every time they try to straighten up and move forward, they feel the boulder pulling them back down. They view their situation as hopeless. Each day gets worse than the last.

For example, let's consider someone who was in an automobile accident and ends up paralyzed from the waist down. Unable to embrace his new reality, this victim starts asking all the WHY questions.

Why did this happen to me?

Why would God take away my legs?

Why should I have to go through life like this?

Why would anyone want to be with me now?

The depression starts to build, the self-esteem falls, and the downward spiral begins. This person withdraws from society and stops taking calls or visits from friends. Maybe he never gets out of bed all day. His depression fills his mind, hour by hour by hour. He has no goals anymore. His will to move on is gone. At this point, his tragedy has become such an enormous boulder that he's down flat under it, squashed by it, with no options, no support system, and only a huge mound of self-pity. The burden of his tragedy is never going to go away.

The only thing that can save this man is his decision to carry this burden in a different way. Anything can trigger his decision—the words of a family member, a speaker he hears, something he sees on the television. But only he himself can choose to carry the burden in a different way.

For someone else, maybe the burden looks more like a huge, heavy anchor chained to their body. They know they should probably move forward, but they feel that the anchor is firmly attached. They're moored to their misery. These people go through the motions of life as if they're in the movie *Groundhog Day*, where they're repeating the same day over and over. To the outside world, things seem fine, but inside, it's a whole other story.

Sometimes you see this anchoredness in someone who has lost his or her significant other. They never deal with the grief. They try to pretend the loss never happened. They push their feelings deep inside and refuse to move on with their life. To their friends and family, they put up a false front and walk around with a smile on their face. They fake being happy, but they're merely going through the normal routines of life on autopilot. Get up, go to work, come home, cook a meal, go to sleep, get up, repeat, repeat, repeat. It seems like they're moving forward, but the reality is that they're stuck in place. That anchor won't let them move. They're stuck in their memories. They wallow in their own misery but show the world a different face. These people need to realize that while God can restore what is lost, what he wants to give them is the strength to move on. They need to trust in him and cherish their memories, but not get stuck in them. That's how they can unchain themselves, drop that anchor, and sail forward.

As for me, I did not want to be carrying a boulder or chained to an anchor. I wanted to be seen as a victor, not a victim. Prior to the shooting, I heard Joel Osteen use that line. It is so true. With God's help, I survived my tragedy. With God's strength, I overcame the lifeless body that I woke up to in the hospital. With God's compassion, I conquered the feelings of despair and hopelessness that I met every day while healing and grieving.

I didn't want a boulder or an anchor. I wanted a medal for courage under fire. That's when I started thinking about the military. If a soldier does something heroic or survives an injury, we give him a medal. Veterans and those on active duty have to live with the burden of what they found in battle, but they wear their medals with pride as survivors and victors. They are not given medals simply because they wear the uniform. They earn them. They deserve them.

When you see a high-level general, you'll see a chest full of medals and ribbons on his uniform. The Medal of Honor, Distinguished Service medals, the Legion of Merit. The Silver Star is awarded to a U.S. service member who shows valor in the face of the enemy. When an American soldier is wounded in battle, he or she is given the Purple Heart for dedication, patriotism, and commitment. These medals show that the wearers have overcome great challenges.

I decided that since I have to carry my burden with me for the rest of my life, I choose to carry it as a medal and proudly wear it on my chest. There's no real, literal medal, of course, yet I can see it every time I look in the mirror. I hope that others can also see it when they hear me speak about overcoming my adversity. I am proud to have survived. I crave opportunities to give hope to others by telling my story as an example of survival.

Surviving that tragic incident gave me a true feeling of self-worth. God allowed me to survive, but he also tested the limits of my character, and I feel that I'm a stronger person now. I know it was God's hand that helped me every single day I lay in that hospital day or struggled to use sleeping muscles. Although many people supported me during my recovery, in the end, I'm the one who had to get out of bed every day and learn how to talk and walk and write again.

I feel not only like I survived the tragedy but that I also conquered the recovery process. I regained my confidence through hard work. My faith, commitment, and dedication to the one true God never wavered. I earned my medal, and I want people to see it. I know that God is proud of me for earning that medal. He's the commander-in-chief that gave it to me. Now I want to help others find their medals.

There is no option for me *not* to help others find their medals. It's a command from God that comes from the Bible. When I looked for a source of inspiration for how to deal with my burden, I found it in Matthew 11: 28-30 (NIV): "Come to me, all you who are weary and burdened, and I will give you rest. Take my yoke upon you and learn from me, for I am gentle and humble in heart, and you will find rest for your souls. For my yoke is easy and my burden is light."

This message is equally inspirational when it is given in modern, everyday English. "Are you tired? Worn out?

Come to me. Get away with me and you'll recover your life. I'll show you how to take a real rest. Walk with me and work with me—watch how I do it. Learn the unforced rhythms of grace. I won't lay anything heavy or ill-fitting on you. Keep company with me and you'll learn to live freely and lightly" (Matthew 11:28-30, *The Message*).

My pastor, Troy Gramling, gives weekly messages like this that have always resonated with me. I started going to Potential Church in 2006 and still go there regularly. Now Pastor Troy's messages have even greater meaning. God, he teaches, does not want us to be dragged down by the burdens we have to carry. Instead, God wants us to learn to live freely and lightly. He wants us to be proud of the person he created us to be. Most importantly, he wants us to share our stories with others who need encouragement.

As I said earlier, during these last few years I have met many other people who are wearing medals of survival. After I give my speeches about survival, people come right up to me. They can't wait to tell me their own stories. It always amazes me how inspiring I find their stories to be, even though I've heard hundreds of stories by now. The reason is simple. Before these people even open their mouths, I can see their medals. I can see it in their body language and in their eyes. When they talk, I can hear it in their voice. Most importantly, I can feel it in their passion.

At the same time, it pains me when I hear someone speaking in that soft voice that shows they think I'm some fragile victim, ready to crumble. *Can't they see my medal?* I figuratively try to puff out my chest to give them a better view. I try to put them at ease about my situation and assure them that I am doing well. I tell them how excited I am about all of the wonderful things going on in my life. I tell them my plans for the future.

And if that doesn't work, I have no problem taking off the medal and speaking frankly. I am usually very open about my thoughts and feelings, and I will often talk about how some people carry boulders and feel crushed or are dragged down by anchors and are nearly drowning in their miseries. I want my listeners to realize that I am not one of those people.

I know that it's not in every person's nature to be so open about their situation, but each person can find his/her way to display the medal. When God gives you something so precious, why would you want to hide it from the world? He wants you to show off your medal.

I accept that society views what happened to me as a tragedy, but I choose not to identify it as a catastrophic tragedy. Instead, I chose to view it as a moment of victorious tragedy. Change is inevitable. It often helps to embrace the change and celebrate the journey itself rather than just the end of the journey. We also need to keep an eye out for the next incredible journey. You need to celebrate each small victory that occurs on the journey.

You have choices. You can choose a lengthy course of pain and grieving. You can get stuck in anger, fear, or depression. You can blame other people for your loss. You can blame yourself. You can choose to give up on life. Although you didn't ask for the burden, you have the right to choose to carry it in a negative way. I just don't recommend assuming a boulder or an anchor because they're heavy. They'll pull you back from joy.

Since I have the ability to choose how I carry my burden, I choose to view the shooting as something that has empowered and challenged me. Using what I have learned during my recovery, I now wear my medal with pride. I understand deep love, deep passion, and deep peace. I move forward with a renewed appreciation and understanding of every aspect of life. I ask for neither pity nor sympathy. Instead, I just ask you to admire my medal.

Chapter Seventeen:

Dealing with Loss. The Incredible Trip

One of the things that people always ask me is how I could move on after losing my wife. As if I needed reminding, they point out that I always spoke about how much I loved Lisa and how happy we were in our marriage Some people can't understand how I can even consider remarrying or having a new family. Others asked if I were simply masking the pain, putting on a happy face to trick people into thinking everything was just dandy. At first, I used to go into lengthy explanations about how I felt and what was truly important to me in life. Then I came up with a new response.

When people ask me how I coped with losing Lisa, I ask them what was one of their favorite trips they ever took in their lives. I have heard many different responses, but usually they involve a wonderful honeymoon or a sentimental vacation to a scene of their childhood. For simplicity sake, let's use the examples of a two-week trip to Italy or a weekend stay at Grandma's house when they were young.

I start by asking them to describe the trip. What did they like about it? It's always interesting to hear about sights, sounds, smells, and feelings. I often feel like they're taking me along on their trip. They smile as they tell specific stories related to that vacation. Sometimes they start laughing as they tell me about a funny adventure on that trip. Maybe it's the winding staircase up to the top of the Leaning Tower of Pisa. Or they'll describe the mouth-watering, thick sauce that covered the pasta they ate at Piazza Navona in Rome. They might describe the steep cliffs with their beautiful, colored houses lining the Amalfi Coast, with the blue waves crashing on the rocks below.

If they're describing their grandmother's house, they might tell me about the antique vases that lined the shelves in the living room. I might hear about the stuffed pork chops and scalloped potatoes that Grandma pulled out of the oven for dinner, followed by the sweet scent of homemade chocolate chip cookies for dessert. Or I hear about the hard candies that Grandma always had in her purse. What wonderful memories.

After hearing about Italy or Grandma, I point out what a lovely trip it was to give the speaker such great memories. But, I ask, what would happen if Italy went bankrupt and shut its doors to any future tourists? What if Grandma's house burned down one day? The typical response is, "What do you mean?"

So I elaborate. "If you were never able to visit Italy again or step inside your Grandma's house again, does that mean that you'd lose the memory of these amazing trips?"

At this point, they start to see where I'm headed with the analogy. I was blessed to have taken a wonderful, four-year journey with Lisa. I have incredible memories, plus sights, smells, sounds, and feelings from that "trip." I laughed a great deal with Lisa along the way. Our laughter left me with a warm feeling inside.

I learned many things during my journey with her. I was, and am, blessed to have such a wonderful marriage, and I know this is a blessing that few people ever get to experience. I can close my eyes any time I want to and imagine our great "trip" together, and nobody can ever take that away from me. So why would I focus on the fact that the trip is over? It's better to appreciate the memories of the journey we had together.

When I was in the hospital, my father asked me an innocent question that summed it all up. He asked me if I would do it all over again with Lisa from the start if I knew this was going to be the outcome. I didn't hesitate to respond. In fact, the answer came out of my mouth almost before the question ended.

"Of course, I'd do it again. There was not a doubt in my mind. It was truly a wonderful journey."

Back to the analogy. It almost sounds too easy. If you knew Italy would shut its doors to tourists in five years, would you still want to go there for a two-week vacation today? As a kid, if you knew Grandma's house would burn down twenty years from now, would that knowledge keep you from staying there for a weekend or eating her chocolate chip cookies or climbing the trees in her back yard?

If those unfortunate events did ultimately happen, would you celebrate every year on the date Italy closed its doors? Would you celebrate on the day Grandma's house burned down? Of course not!

You might feel sad that you can never have those experiences again, but you still have your memories of them. You can still remember what Italy looked like. You can still remember Grandma's living room and kitchen. Your experiences became part of you, part of your character and your personal makeup. What you had and did cannot be lost.

What I want you to remember is that I do not want to lament the fact that a journey ended and I can never go back. Yes, Lisa is gone. No, I can't bring her back. But, yes, I can rejoice in having had the opportunity to take such an incredible trip with her. When the anniversary of the tragedy comes around, I don't mourn. On the first anniversary, I left the country and went to visit friends so I could create new memories. I wanted to keep moving forward with my life.

There is a commonly accepted process that most therapists will tell you about when you're dealing with a great loss. As given in Elizabeth Kübler-Ross's book, *On Death and Dying*, grief has five stages: denial, anger, bargaining, depression, and acceptance. Not everyone passes through these five stages in the same order, and you might go back and forth between the various stages, but the idea is that we must experience the pain of the loss and then try to move forward with our lives. I take it one step further by suggesting that we should not try to "get over it," but instead celebrate the fact that we had the opportunity to take this journey and create such amazing memories. I would rather celebrate those parts of the journey that were wondrous and joyful. When I tell stories about Lisa or our marriage, I don't dwell on how it ended. I focus on the wonderful stories and memories that made the journey so exciting. Then I turn my attention toward the future and look at the next chapters of my life with hopeful anticipation.

Understandably, different people will have different timeframes for being able to appreciate their wonderful memories and moving forward. When the emotion is raw and the feelings of pain are still fresh, it's hard to celebrate the wonderful journey you took with that person. What I'm suggesting is that at some point it's healthy to be thankful that you were able to have the deceased person in your life. Only after grieving according to your personal timetable might you be able to move forward.

There are also times when God puts people in your life to show you that it's okay to move on. After one of my speeches, for example, I met a young woman and we exchanged many emails of support for each other. She initially wasn't going to come hear me speak that Sunday morning because she didn't want to have one more person say, "Move on." Like me in the hospital, she had heard enough people telling her to look on the bright side of things.

However, something told her to come that morning. She believes it was God nudging her out the door. She was a cancer survivor, and her current suffering dealt with the loss of her husband and soul mate. He had passed away around the same time as Lisa. After my speech, this woman came up to me, and we shared some nice words. She was open and receptive to my message and shared intimate details with me.

We both learned quite a bit from each other that morning about how to move on. Not only did she inspire me with her story, but she also had unwavering support for me when I told her that I was starting to date again. Within a month, she wrote to me again and told me that after hearing about my dates, she felt less guilty, and now she, too, was starting to date. We were both in the same shoes; I needed her support and she needed me to encourage her and say it was okay for her to move on.

Shortly after she began dating again, she started to email me with some concerns. Because of the way her husband had died in his sleep, she was overly concerned whenever her kids or her new boyfriend fell asleep. She told me she sat there, watching their chests go up and down, scared that they would stop breathing. She was feeling anxious and having difficult thoughts about her other loved ones dying. I reminded her of my speech and told her that God had already thrown the towel in for her. After she had survived cancer and the death of her spouse, there was no way that God was going to give her any more burdens to carry. Her anxious thoughts were proof of the fact that she was at her limit. I reminded her that this was all just strength training from the greatest strength coach that she could imagine. Then I also reminded her that she needed to just appreciate the fact that she had been able to have her husband in her life for so many years and that he had given her two beautiful children. Now, I added, it was time for her to appreciate the journey, lose the bad memories of how it ended, and step forward with her life. She agreed and said she felt much better with this new mind-set.

We have been conditioned to label certain events as "tragic" or "catastrophic," but sometimes bad things just happen. It is what it is, and you cannot read too much into it. With the loss of a loved one, we sometimes feel that there has to be a certain amount of grief and suffering to show that we're showing respect.

But those who pass on do not require that we suffer their passing. Sometimes we create additional, unnecessary, pain so that we can feel like we've adequately grieved for the departed. Each stage of life brings with it new people, new opportunities, and new blessings. It's a wonderful thing if someone can share several stages of your life, but if that's not possible for some reason, then it's good to be able to cherish them for being in our lives as long as they were there.

Another example. When you finished grade school, you had great memories. But you were looking forward to high school and making new friends and having some new experiences. When you graduated from high school, it was the same. You were looking forward to college or work. It's a cycle that is repeated many times in your life.

The people in your life and the experiences you enjoy with them help to form your character. They will not be forgotten because they are a part of you. Bits of them can be seen in you as you move forward in life. You always have the memories of a loved one and the great journey you had together.

Keep in mind that your memories can never stop you from taking a new journey and creating new memories (maybe even with a new person). I don't view life as one big journey but as a series of small journeys that all lead us eventually to him who created us.

Chapter Eighteen:
The Importance of a Positive Attitude

People often come up to me and ask how I learned to be so positive after all I've gone through. They want to know how they can change their attitude and be more positive. I quickly point out to them that the positive attitude must be there before the tragedy if there's any chance of its surviving after the tragedy. For me, having a positive attitude was always my way of life. It helped me get through the shooting and its aftermath.

I know that it's easy to tell people to be more positive. It's easy to tell people to look on the bright side. It's easy to say, "Just see the glass as half full." The reality is that many people struggle with being positive. Some of them call themselves "realists" and see no reason to be optimistic or positive. Many times, they laugh sarcastically at you for being "the eternal optimist," and they're quick to point out that there are no guarantees in life, that bad things happen regardless of how positive you are.

Maybe so, but anyone who learns to be more consistently positive will have a better chance of surviving tragic episodes as they go through the recovery process. Moreover, we must try to develop this positive attitude now, before tragedy strikes. There are many ways you can accomplish this goal.

My first suggestion is to cherish every moment of your life. We spend so much time running from event to event. We worry about deadlines and upcoming meetings. We stress over work assignments and childcare issues. We get frustrated with family members and friends. We've become experts at working ourselves into a frenzy about the stressful situations in our lives.

What amazes me is that people have no problem reciting a list of stressors they currently have in their lives, but can they similarly rattle off a list of cherished moments? Even from their last few weeks? I have always tried to stop, be present, and enjoy the moment. Since waking up from that coma, I feel mandated to, as they say, stop and smell the roses. When I see a beautiful sunset on the way home from work, for example, I take time to acknowledge it. When my wife greets me at the door with a kiss, I stop to appreciate that kiss. When I come into the office and my coworkers greet me with a smile, I enjoy that moment, too. When I hit every green light on the way to work, I get excited about my good fortune. Cherishing all those little moments in your life adds up to a greater appreciation of life as a whole. That will lead to a more positive attitude.

It is truly important that you count your blessings every day. When I hear people complain about their salary or that their car didn't start this morning, or that they have some other problem, I ask them to focus on the great things in their lives, on their blessings. These blessings might include having a roof over your head and food on your table each night. Having a smart, healthy child. Being able to breathe without a respirator and having two legs that work. Living in a free country where anything is possible if you work hard. Of course, these don't apply to everyone, but if you know the person who is complaining, you should be able to tell them a hundred blessings in their life for each little complaint they have.

In my office, I have always used one little activity with my secretary to put us both in the right mindset every day. Each day, we both say out loud three things we are thankful for in the last twenty-four hours. It can be as big as "I got a raise" or as little as "my daughter came back to the car to give me another kiss before she went into the school." The only rules are that it has to be a positive thing we're grateful for and we can't say the exact same thing the next day. It helps us get to know each other better, it helps us focus on the positive blessings in our lives, and it always reduces the stress level in the office.

In addition to counting my blessings, I still celebrate small victories, too. When I get out of a chair now, I feel joy in my heart at how easy it is for me to stand up without a struggle. When I come in from a hot, sunny day and enjoy a bottle of cold water, I think back to those four months when I could have no water in my mouth and savor every drop of water that now goes down my throat. When I walk down stairs, I remember how it would take me ten to twenty seconds per step when

165

I first started learning how to walk up and down stairs again. Those pity-parties feel like they occurred decades ago because now I have victory parties every single day.

I also believe that it's important that you tell and show others that you love them. Life is short and precious. We don't have time to wait until it's too late to let others feel our love. It's important to not only tell them that you love them, but tell them *why* you love them. Be specific about what qualities you admire about your loved ones or what specific moments you appreciate from your life together with that person.

Words, of course, are not enough by themselves. You need to show others how much you love them through your actions. Pick up the telephone and call them to find out how they're doing. Better yet, make a lunch date to see them face-to-face and share stories. Make their birthday special by giving them a meaningful gift or sending them a note with an article enclosed that you think might be of interest to them. Hug them, hold them, kiss them, touch them. The human touch is essential to showing others you love them.

When you experience a tragedy, people will come out of the woodwork to support you in the beginning. Even casual acquaintances will feel compelled to show you support at the beginning of your time of need. They will call you, email you, write to you, come over and see you. After a few months, however, some of these people won't know what else to do. Or they'll get busy again with their own lives. This is completely understandable.

As the days stretch on after tragedy, it can be easy for you to settle into your own thoughts and daily routine and forget about those who truly love and support you. The phone calls, emails, and texts come in with less frequency. Despite your thoughts being focused inward, this is when you must make some effort to stay in contact with those who want to shower you with love and support. You don't always have to wait for them to contact you. Pick up the phone and call them. Tell them how much you appreciate their love and support, especially at one of your darkest hours. Send a text or an email. Post a little note on Facebook so people know you're still alive and doing well. Thank people for what they've done for you. People who love you sometimes need to know that their actions and support mean something to you. Tell them!

I have a new appreciation for my parents and brothers. My parents selflessly gave five months of their lives to watch over me and help me in my recovery. When my brother Brian took over my finances, I gave him a power of attorney to make sure that all my expenses were paid, my accounts were up to date, and the insurance claims for health and disability were timely made. My brother Kerry flew in from Chicago many times just to give me support in person. I told them all what this attention meant to me.

Another thing you can do to keep a positive attitude is to surround yourself with people that truly are rooting for you. This is as easy to do as when I stopped by the ICU at St. Mary's Hospital or visited the Mt. Sinai Rehab Center, where I learned how to walk again, to thank my caregivers. I've visited the ICU on several occasions since I woke up in February, 2010. It's about an hour and a half drive for me, so I don't get up to West

Palm Beach very often, but if I ever need a pick-me-up, there is no better place for me to go than the place where my miracle happened. After all, I am one of the biggest victories those nurses and doctors who contributed to my miraculous recovery can claim. I make sure that I go back, at the very least, every February 24, which is the day I woke up.

The first time I walked back into the ICU, about six months after I woke up, most of the nurses didn't recognize me. That's because I was walking. I walked up to the nurses station and looked right into the eyes of one of the nurses who had cared for me.

"Can I help you?" she asked.

"Hi, Stephanie," I said in my most winsome voice. "Remember me?"

This nurse, who had seen me naked and vulnerable when she gave me sponge baths and tended to all the tubes, looked up at me and studied my face. She looked right into my eyes. I could see the wheels spinning as she tried to identify me. All of a sudden, it clicked. Her mouth dropped open. She practically hurdled the desk to come around and give me a big hug. She called two other nurses over.

"Frank, Paul, come here right away! You are not going to believe who's here to visit us. You won't believe it!"

As the two other nurses came toward us, they were smiling at me in the way you smile when you are supposed to know someone but you cannot quite place their face. Neither one was quite sure what to say.

Then, just like with Stephanie, it clicked, and they stumbled over each other to see who could hug me first.

One by one, nurses and doctors came over to see me, and each of them had their own mixture of emotions. Some had tears and some seemed confused, but they all had big smiles, too.

What I said earlier is true. *I am one of their greatest victories.* The nurses confirmed this when they told me that they see so many people that don't make it. That's because the ICU has the sickest, most badly injured patients in the hospital. Many of these people die. Others recover, but not fully.

To see someone who was as far gone as me come walking back into the ICU six months later was not only their reward, but also a justification for what they do every day in their jobs. For me, the best part of the visit was that it made me feel good to show them how grateful I was (and still am) that they never gave up on me. They kept telling me that I cheated death, that I am an inspiration. Talk about creating positive energy.

The same thing happened when I went to Mt. Sinai Rehabilitation Center a year after I was released. When I walked down the hallway, none of the therapists recognized me. I walked right up to them, looked them in the face. Our eyes locked. I did a little dance, right there in front of them. I even brought a picture book that showed my recovery in 2010 and left a copy there at the rehab center for the other therapists to see, too. When they recognized me, they were so delighted, and their delight filled me with a tremendously positive attitude.

In my visits, I also remembered Alfredo Bless and how he had filled me with his positive energy at our first meeting. Alfredo and I have stayed good friends and see each other every few months when I have a chance to get up to Palm Beach. When he's down in the dumps, I remind him of the lessons that he taught me. Now we support each other.

Having my friends and family in my life is wonderful, but when I need a different kind of support, these visits to the ICU, the rehab, or to see Alfredo give me another perspective and a different kind of love. Sometimes, I get encouragement simply by hearing the stories of other people who have overcome tragedy. It has all helped me to move forward with my new reality.

Your supporters might be members of your church, people you have met who are in a similar situation, or former classmates that learned about your tragedy and prayed for you during your time of need. It's not hard to find these people. They are typically the ones who are sending you encouraging letters and emails.

On some days, however, there may be no one there to give you the support you need. At these times, you need to learn how to become your own cheerleader. In Chapter 15, I talked about getting off your stool and how you had to be the one to get yourself out of bed every day. There are definitely going to be days when you are mad, sad, and depressed. That's when you need to motivate yourself, set goals, and accomplish them. In the beginning, you can set small goals that you can accomplish fairly quickly and easily. For example, I tried to increase my walking by fifty feet each time I went out. I worked on learning how to put on my own bandages. And of course, each time I reached one of these small goals, I celebrated another victory. As I improved, I set larger goals, but I always reminded myself that I was progressing, and with each victory, my new reality looked brighter and more achievable.

I have also found it very helpful to encourage other people who are struggling. I sometimes meet these people after I give one of my speeches, but there are times in everyday life when my story might come up and people feel compelled to share the burdens they're carrying. By listening to their stories, showing compassion, staying strong for them, and giving them encouraging words, I can keep myself in a better place mentally.

When I'm listening to others and sharing my story, I feel it is important to confess that I had my pity-parties in the beginning, that I had some dark hours during my recovery. I share the strategies I used for overcoming my pity-parties. I tell them, for example, how I congratulate myself and celebrate a small victory every time I feel a pity-party coming on and I refuse to give in to it. People respond well when they realize that there's hope for them to break out of their funk.

Finally, as you improve your positive attitude, you will be able to smile more. It's healthy to joke around and not take yourself too seriously. I used to laugh at myself when my floppy wrists caused me to do something goofy or when I lost my balance and fell over. I also found that it put other people at ease when I laughed at myself.

You have probably heard that old expression, laughter is the best medicine. I firmly believe that it's true for both physical and mental issues. After tragedy, you don't always feel like laughing, but if you can try to laugh, you will feel better. I watched comedy shows on TV, funny movies, and funny Internet videos. I also gravitated toward any friend who had a good sense of humor.

When the bad feelings started to creep up on me, I let them happen. That's part of the grieving process. But I never felt afraid to enjoy life again. Any time I was laughing was a moment that I wasn't crying, and that was a useful catalyst for restoring my positive attitude. Now when I laugh, I appreciate the fact that I *can* laugh.

In sum, you cannot wait until after the tragedy to start working on your positive attitude. When you're celebrating small victories, counting your blessings, and looking for the good things in your life, you're changing your attitude. When you're telling and showing others how much you love them, you're changing your own energy. When you're helping others who are struggling with their own burdens, you're finding peace in yourself. Don't forget to laugh. If you laugh, the world will laugh with you.

Chapter Nineteen:

Embrace Your Reality —

Envision Your Future

As people go through the process of surviving a tragedy, one of the things they say is that they want to "get their life back." Back to normal, back to like it was before, back to the way it used to be. But that will never happen. At least, not the "normal" we had before our tragedies. Anyone who has gone through a tragedy needs understand that their old life is gone, and what was normal before will not be normal in the future.

You will never be exactly that same person you were before because now you have been through this tragedy, and it's part of you, part of your life experience. You can never go back to the old "normal" because it's likely that this tragedy has changed you in ways you may not even recognize yet. You can never go back to the way you were before.

The good news is that you have a new "normal," and a new life. But before you can begin to move forward, you need to stop comparing the present to the past. Instead, take stock of where you are right now. Imagine how you can move forward, not from any previous starting point, but from where you stand right now. In other words, if you can't walk and never will walk again, it's unproductive to spend all your time wanting to walk the way you used to walk or exercising the way you used to exercise. Be realistic. Where are you right now? What realistic goals can you set for the future? If there is hope that you will be able to walk again, set realistic goals. Focus on being able to walk for 100 feet, then 300 feet, then for half a mile, and so on. Every time you reach a goal, celebrate it. It's a victory for you.

Being realistic does not, however, mean that you should set the bar low. Be positively realistic. Set goals based on your current condition. Envision yourself meeting each goal you set. Visualization is a great motivator when you start to feel depressed or feel that your life is too overwhelming.

For example, if you're focused on learning to walk again, consider finding a 5K race that will happen six months from now. Use this long-term goal to help yourself meet the short-term goal of walking every day. Think about the joy and triumph you will feel when you complete the race. You can also, and more modestly, envision yourself walking back into your office for the first time and seeing all your co-workers cheering for you with balloons and cake.

In my case, I had two future events to look forward to. First, as I wrote earlier, I was scheduled to speak in Japan in November, 2010. This speech had been booked just prior to the shooting, and after I woke up, it was still far enough in the future that I hoped to be able to walk on stage. Lying in my hospital bed, unable to talk, I daydreamed about the moment I would walk on stage in Osaka. I could see the audience. I could hear them applauding and cheering. I must have daydreamed about this event every single day of the five weeks I spent in the ICU. I knew I had a lot to relearn. I also had to practice learning how to talk and move my hands. On days when I was frustrated about how the words were coming out of my mouth, I would stop, take a deep breath, and try again. As speaking improved, I began to work on putting energy behind my words. I always tell people that the best speakers and trainers are those that can fill a room with energy. Although my energetic speaking might have seemed strange to the nurses and people who visited me, I was working up to my speech in Japan.

The second event was a greater physical challenge. During one visit, my brother Brian mentioned a running and biking race called Muddy Buddy, which was to take place in Miami in December, 2010. He and I had participated in the 2009 race in Chicago, and now, within three weeks of my waking up, Brian told me that he signed us up for the race in Miami.

I laughed, but as I started to improve, I decided to set this race as a second goal. I didn't know if I would really be able to do it, but when I was lying in the hospital bed and envisioning myself competing in the race and crossing the finish line, just the visualization gave me the will power to keep fighting to recover.

After I left the hospital and had to practice walking on my own, I kept motivating myself by visualizing, first, walking on the stage in Osaka and, second, participating in that Muddy Buddy Race. I felt the wind blowing on my face as I crossed the finish line, I visualized the sights, heard the sounds, smelled the smells, felt the feelings I would have at the event.

By setting the bar high, I kept myself motivated to get out of bed. For anyone who is recovering from a major illness or injury, I suggest that you find a future event that you can use as a goal. Make it a realistic goal—you may not be running a full marathon very soon—but set the bar as high as possible. Knowing that you have a deadline forces you to get up and get better.

Another strategy for dealing with the mental challenge of a recovery is realizing that sometimes things just don't make sense. Prior to my incident, I had always acknowledged the fact that life isn't always fair. Sometimes people get promoted before you do, even though they don't deserve it. Sometimes people who are unethical or cheat seem to get ahead and never get caught. Once you realize that things in life aren't always fair, it's easier to be content with the blessings you have in your life.

After my tragedy, this concept of fairness grew. During my initial pity-parties, I kept asking *Why me? Why did this happen to me?* It was unfair that it happened to me. I didn't deserve it. It didn't make sense. It wasn't fair that Lisa was dead. It wasn't fair that I couldn't move or talk. It wasn't fair that I had to go through so much grieving and physical recovery at the same time.

About a year after I recovered, a friend heard me speak and suggested that when I wrote this book, I should tell in detail how mad I must have been during physical therapy and how upset I was that I had been shot, how unhappy I was that this had happened to me. What I told him was that by the time I was in therapy, the pity-parties were over. I wasn't mad anymore, nor was I still feeling sorry for myself. By that point, I had realized that an unfair thing had happened to me and what I needed to focus on were the blessings in my life. I was moving forward.

Of course, even though I had moved past my pity-parties, other people constantly affected my mood during the recovery and my grieving process with some of the things they said. It's amazing how insensitive some people can be. God "had a plan" for me, they said, or I had to "look for the good" in this catastrophe. Before my tragedy, I myself had always struggled to find the right thing to say to someone who had just lost a loved one or been through some kind of tragedy. After my own tragedy, I realized that almost everyone is tongue-tied. They don't know what to say. Yes, most people were honestly trying to make me feel better, but they had no idea that I didn't want to hear that I should "feel lucky that I survived" or that Lisa was "in a better place." One priest even told me that, if I married again, I should name my first child Lisa to preserve her memory.

Thanks to all the media coverage, other people treated me like a mini-celebrity. One nurse assistant in the rehab hospital came into my room, and the first thing she said: "I know you! I've seen you on TV." She was as giddy as if she'd met someone really famous.

It made me feel awkward because she only knew me because of the tragedy, which was the lowest point of my life.

I don't know if not knowing what to say is universal, but here are the only things I wanted to hear from visitors: (1) I'm sorry for your loss, (2) I have been thinking of you, (3) Your family is in my prayers, and (4) If you need anything, I'm here for you.

What is the lesson here? Don't try to be philosophical or tell a victim that "everything is for the best." Instead of offering platitudes, offer to do errands for the person, bring a hot meal, or take care of other simple tasks that will make their lives easier during the difficult times.

For every person, who said something inappropriate to me, however, there were five people that said or did just the right thing. My family, the nurses, and the therapists were wonderful every step of the way. My friends and coworkers really came out to support me. Sometimes, it was the smallest gesture that helped me keep moving forward with my recovery, and for those small gestures, I am eternally grateful.

Examples. My friend Anita stopped by regularly, even for five minutes, after court hearings in downtown Miami and told me funny stories or office gossip. My buddy Josh called me every other day and brought me smoothies. If I told him I was tired, he stayed only a couple minutes. My friend Sonny and her daughter Cindy baked my favorite cookies to bring on their first visit, then brought me a box of drinking straws on their second visit because they saw I had difficulty lifting a glass. My secretary Maria went out of her way to visit me and fill me in on what was happening with certain legal files or tell me about trials on my cases while I was sleeping. Mario, a coworker, brought me a DVD player and a bunch of movies to watch. Victor, my boss, was wonderful with my parents while I was sleeping and assured me that my job would be waiting when I was ready to come back. The owner of the insurance company, Mr. Parrillo, made it a point to personally follow up with me when I finally returned to work. To this day, I feel blessed to work for people that care about me.

More examples. My old boss, Dan, and his wife Donna came to visit me, along with Sharon, a former coworker, and her husband Richard. It was obvious from the moment they entered my room that they cared about me and were rooting for me to get back on my feet. They were my very own cheerleaders. My friends Todd, Adi, Jane, and Roger brought a four-course meal to my rehab room and stayed all evening, hanging out just like we had so many times before. After I got out of rehab, my friend Annie invited me over for home-cooked meals so that I was eating something healthy that tasted good. My buddy Michael came over with a home-cooked meal, too; this one was curried chicken, which his wife Susana had cooked for me. My friend Beth and her daughter Maria came to my condo and taught me how to cook for myself, given my new restrictions. There was no shortage of good meals sent my way each week.

Hernando, a friend of mine from JCI, came back from the JCI Conference of the Americas in Argentina with video messages from about thirty of my friends. Shortly thereafter, I went down to the Florida Keys with my buddies, Mike, Joe, and Pete, plus a bunch of other guys, for a get-away that just made me feel like all was right in the world. Even friends from far away, like Lori, Soli, and Kirsten, plus many JCI friends around the world sent love and positive energy via phone or email. It is truly amazing what people will do to help you get to a good place in your mind. I am convinced that God had previously placed all these people in my life as a support system to help me through my recovery and to move forward with my new life.

Although it is important to embrace your new reality, there are times when your friends just want to treat you with kid gloves and walk on egg shells around you. Tragedy is an uncomfortable word for most people, and they can seldom cope with severe tragedy. As you're trying to celebrate victories small and large and keep a positive attitude, you might be begging your friends and family to just treat you like they've always treated you, but even for people trained to deal with tragedy and loss, this can be difficult. The first time people see you after your tragedy is the most awkward. When I was in the ICU, only family members could visit me. Once I moved to the rehabilitation facility in Miami, however, I was inundated by friends and coworkers who wanted to see me. At first, I thought all these visits were going to be wonderful, but I quickly found out that they would be awkward. Some of my closest friends later confessed that they had struggled to decide what they were going to say or do when they first saw me. I had to learn how to put them at ease right from the start. I learned quickly that joking around with them helped, but if they still felt uneasy, I simply told them how happy I was that they were there and treating me like a normal person because other people had been treating me like a baby. This usually allowed us to fall back into our old routines of just being us.

Once I was back to work and my daily routine, I wanted one place that seemed normal to me. My condo wasn't normal yet because, although all of Lisa's clothing and other items had been removed, I often had no idea where things was because Lisa had been the one who knew where most things were in the condo, and then my parents lived there for several weeks while I was in the ICU. I felt out of place in my own home.

The one place that felt normal was my office at the law firm. During my time in the coma, my office had been boxed up and sent to my brother's house because they were uncertain if I would ever be back. But three weeks after leaving rehab, when I transported my boxes back to the office, I put every piece of paper back in the same folder and in the same drawer where it had been before. I hung up my diplomas in the exact same places on the walls. It became the one place in the world that was exactly the same after the incident as before. This gave me a sense of security, which was exactly what I needed.

Embracing my new reality was therefore a combination of several things. First, I envisioned my new future from a new starting point. Second, I set goals to help me stay motivated. Third, I realized that life is not always fair and that I should be content with the blessing I have. Fourth, I allowed my friends and family to do things for me and be involved in my recovery. Finally, after some readjustments, I settled in to my new "normal." I embraced my new reality and began looking forward to my next journey.

Chapter Twenty:

Becoming Fully Aware of Tragedy and Survival

Until we get to live an eternal life of joy in heaven, we have to deal with pain and suffering in this world. Since my incident and recovery, I have become acutely aware of how many people suffer major tragedies every day. More than 100 million people visit the emergency room each year in the United States, and many of those people are there due to a catastrophic accident. Almost every day, I read news stories about shootings where there are multiple fatalities. And there are also other crimes, car accidents, plane crashes, tragic sports injuries, acts of God, and other catastrophic losses.

But it isn't just the victims that I think of when I read these stories. Imagine how many families are affected by tragedy, how many people have gone through the same kind of recovery as me, and even more people who suffered along with the victim of the tragedy, just as my family did. Murder, car accidents, sports injuries, and fires, tornadoes, and floods are part of everyday life, and as a result of my own experience, I see the human side of the story when I hear it on the television or read it in the newspaper. It breaks my heart to see the suffering these people are experiencing. It serves as a constant reminder that I am truly blessed to have survived my own ordeal. As I have traveled and met people with their own stories, I've been inspired. I found this quote that sums up my feelings about these survivors:

> The most beautiful people we have known are those who have known defeat, known suffering, known struggle, known loss, and have found their way out of the depths. These persons have an appreciation, a sensitivity and an understanding of life that fills them with compassion, gentleness, and a deep loving concern. Beautiful people do not just happen.....--Elisabeth Kűbler-Ross

My brother Kerry recently sent me a link to a story written by Michael Vitez in the *Philadelphia Inquirer* about a guy who overcame incredible odds. His name is Matt Miller, and he was a straight-A student and athlete at the University of Virginia. As well as being a star of the swim team, he also trained for triathlons and was an avid runner and bicyclist. One morning, while on an eighty-five-mile training ride, he was involved in a severe accident in which he lost control of his bicycle and swerved into a head-on collision with a Porsche. He was thrown off the bicycle, flew through the air, and landed on the pavement. He barely survived. In fact, in the first seventy-two hours, it looked as though he would not make it. Like me, he was induced into a coma. He was suffering from severe head trauma, and the surgeons needed to cut off the top of his skull to give the brain room to expand because of the swelling. The CT scans and X-rays taken in the hospital showed that every bone in his face had been broken. The doctors felt that there was no way he would have 100 percent of his mental capacity back…*if* he survived.

After Matt woke up, and after the surgery to his face, his mouth was wired shut. Visitors described him as looking deformed, as if he had had a stroke. And yet one of the first things Matt typed on his ICU talk-pad was, "Can I go to physics lab?" This young athlete had a positive attitude. He was already thinking about getting better and moving forward. And his rapid recovery was astounding. He never seemed to have the pity-parties that I and others enjoyed. After his recovery, he went back to doing his triathlons and has thrived in his new reality. Matt got "off his stool" even faster than I did. This is the kind of story that should be told all over America rather than the negative news we always hear.[1]

While doing research for a speech, I also came across the story of Arthur Renowitzy.[2] Arthur was shot point-blank outside a San Francisco night club by someone he didn't know and never saw again. He was rushed to the hospital, where he, too, was medically induced into

---

1   Michael Vitez, "A swerve, a crash – 'That boy's dead'." (*Philadelphia Inquirer*. 21 June 2009).

2   See www.lifegoesonfoundation.org.

a coma for twenty-three days. He survived the shooting, but when he awoke, he was paralyzed from the chest down and was told that he would never walk again. He was eighteen at the time of the shooting, a young man just starting out with his life.

After he was released from his rehabilitation, he entered into a severe depression and spent several weeks in his bedroom, twenty-four hours a day with tinfoil on his windows. He was debating suicide until his father and brother forced him out of the house to try hand cycling. He then met a wheelchair basketball coach and found his new passion. Although he was now in a wheelchair, he decided to make the most of his life and move forward with the realization that life must go on. He now plays for a semi-professional wheelchair basketball team called the San Jose Spokes. Arthur had made a decision during his recovery that he would embrace his new reality rather than spiral into depression.

He also established the Life Goes On Foundation, whose aim is to help bring an end to gun violence among young people in California. Arthur does not want to see another young person become a victim of gun violence. Today he runs the foundation and hits the streets, speaking about his incident and spreading his message of peace. He also speaks at special events. Like me, Arthur had people in his corner giving him encouragement, but it was his decision to get back into the ring.

I don't just see such stories in print, on line, or on TV. I seem to find people with inspiring stories everywhere I turn. While taking the sworn statement of a man who had been in a motor vehicle accident, I learned that eight months before this minor accident, he had been involved in a horrific automobile crash in which he sustained massive injuries. He was a twenty-nine-year-old man with an amazing attitude. I could see the medal on his chest the minute he walked through the door. When he told the story of his crash and his recovery, he seemed very proud of his survival and recovery. He told me that after the crash he had been found unconscious on the roadway by the police. He had suffered a major head trauma and was rushed to the emergency room. In the ICU, he was in a coma for seventy days. In addition to the brain injury in his frontal lobe, he suffered a collapsed lung and had other complications in his torso. He described his painstaking rehabilitation, where (like me) he had to learn to stand up, walk, and even use the bathroom again. I told him I completely understood. He gave me a funny look at first, but when I shared my story with him after we'd completed the sworn statement, it was like we had an instant bond. We shook hands and told each other how blessed we were to be alive. This man had the right attitude. and he was as happy to display his medal on his chest as I was to display mine.

Today, as I read the newspapers and watch CNN, the stories of tragedy touch me in a different way. My senses are heightened. I watched in horror in 2011 as the Norwegian Massacre was reported. The gunman, Anders Behring Breivik dressed himself in a police uniform and worked his way into a youth camp for the Workers Youth League, an affiliate of the Norwegian Labor

Party. This youth camp was attended by approximately 600 teenagers. He identified himself as a police officer and indicated that he was there for a routine check due to a possible bomb threat. After getting people to gather around him closely, he pulled out his guns and started shooting indiscriminately into the crowd. The youth camp was being held on an island, so over a hundred young people were trapped in the line of fire. Sixty-nine young people were murdered, and sixty-six others were severely injured. The gunman even shot at people who were trying to escape the island by swimming across the lake. Survivors described a scene of terror where some victims begged for their lives and many others pretended to be dead in order to escape execution.

As I read that last detail, it brought back vivid memories of when I was lying perfectly still as the killer ran past me into the little girl's room because I was so terrified that he would stop and shoot me again. How many victims from the incident in Norway will have to relive their memories of playing dead? How many families are still suffering from the loss of loved ones?

In March of 2011 came one of the worst natural disasters in modern history, an 8.9 magnitude earthquake in Japan followed by a tsunami and a meltdown in a nuclear power plant. Together, these caused tremendous damage. In that incident, there were 15,845 confirmed deaths and 5,893 injuries, and 3,380 people are still missing. That means that there are 25,000 families who are still suffering in Japan.

Even after going through my own tragedy, I have difficulty grasping the magnitude of those numbers. It is another reminder that there are always people in this world who have it worse situation than whatever we're going through, and reading about the disaster made me immediately stop and pray for the victims and their families. My prayer of course was that God would give them strength.

By Christmas day of 2011, I was already two years post-tragedy and my life was back on track. Whenever I hear about catastrophic tragedies that occur on major holidays, the news still strikes close to my heart and makes me even more sympathetic. On December 25, 2011, I saw two headlines that jumped off the screen at me: *Seven Found Dead after Opening Christmas Presents in Fort Worth* and *Christmas Fire Kills Three Children and Parents of a Connecticut Woman.*

The first story touched a nerve because of its similarities to my own story. An estranged husband came to his wife's house on Christmas Day dressed as Santa Claus. He came to see his children on what is normally a joyous day. He sat around with his wife and family, including his two children, and they opened up Christmas presents.

At some point after gifts were opened—and presumably he saw the true joy that children express as they untie the bows, rip open the gift wrapping, and start playing—this husband pulled out a gun and killed the other six people in the room. Then he killed himself. Here is another family where grandparents, aunts and uncles, and friends are left behind, people who will all suffer the consequences of a tragedy none of them could have prevented.

The second story shows what can happen when a person cannot break out of the downward spiral that often follows tragedy. It made me extremely sad for the woman who survived. She was an advertising executive that had just moved into a million-dollar house in Connecticut with her three young daughters. The grandparents of the little girls had come to visit, so the woman had all the important people in her world in one house over the holidays. And in one night, it was all ripped away from her as a fire broke out in the home and the flames were so high and so hot that her daughters and her parents were unable to escape. All five perished that night in the most horrific way. Losing one child would be hard enough, but losing all three would be unbearable.

Typically in these situations, a person would rely on their parents or other family members for support. But this woman also lost her parents in this tragedy. Things got so bad for her that she attempted suicide exactly one month after the tragedy. As I write this, I have read that she is seeking physical and mental treatment. But her collapse shows what can happen after such a catastrophe.

Another national news story that happened nearly a year after I woke up that caught my attention because of its similarities to my situation. On January 8, 2011, United States Congresswoman Gabrielle Giffords and nineteen other people were shot by a crazy gunman who began firing into a crowd during a gathering she was holding for her constituents in Arizona. Six people died, but even though she was shot in the head, Congresswoman

Giffords did not die. She was rushed to the hospital in critical condition with a severe head trauma. There was little hope that she would survive.

Emergency room doctors performed emergency brain surgery on Giffords. They had to extract skull fragments from her brain. The bullet had passed through her head without crossing the midline of her brain. Had the bullet hit the midline of her brain, she would have had much more critical injuries. Doctors placed Giffords in a medically-induced coma to allow her to recover from the brain surgery. When she awoke, she soon realized that she was facing a long road during the recovery. She didn't even know what functions would return as she began physical therapy, which included therapists trying to sit her up in bed and move her legs. She had a tracheotomy tube in her throat to assist with her breathing and had to learn all of her activities of daily living again. These details were so similar to my situation that as I closely followed news reports of her physical therapy, occupational therapy, and speech therapy, I felt like I was reliving my entire recovery. She was going through a nearly identical process.

Giffords' story made me realize that people all over the world are going through therapy and recovery every single day. I watched as she said her first words and read about her learning to write again. I felt such compassion for her because I had been in her shoes and, understanding her frustration, my heart broke for her.

When she arrived at the rehabilitation center, the therapists and doctors were optimistic and felt that she had great rehabilitation potential. Determined to make a full recovery to get back to her job in Congress, she decided to work hard. By April, she had perfect control of her left arm and leg and was able to walk under supervision. I was overjoyed when the news reported that she was able to read again and understand what she read. Then she started to write with her left hand and speak in short phrases. God gave her the strength, and she ran with it.

She continued with her recovery and was relentless in relearning how to do everything. On August 1, 2011, Giffords made an appearance in the U.S. House of Representatives and received a standing ovation. As I watched this, I had the biggest smile I have ever had on my face.

For one moment during a tense debate over the government debt ceiling, all the members of Congress united to give Giffords the recognition that she deserved for overcoming her tragedy. She has never lost focus on moving forward with her new reality.

Since the beginning of time, the world has been filled with tragedy. It will continue to exist all around us in the present and the future. Before I was shot, I saw stories of tragedies, but I never appreciated the suffering that often lasted for years. I never truly understood the losses the families had to deal with or how the survivors had to overcome tremendous odds to live in their new reality.

Now, more than ever, I appreciate the will to survive that so many people exhibit every day after dealing with a tragedy. These stories of survival should be shared again and again so that they give hope to others. I wish there were news stations devoted wholly to sharing these amazing stories. God is great. He will see you through the depths of despair if you trust in him.

Chapter Twenty-One:

Pamela's Story

As I said in the previous chapter, it seemed like everywhere I traveled, I was meeting people with amazing stories. One story that touched me greatly came from a person I met halfway around the world. When I went to Austria to do a weeklong leadership workshop, I met a woman from Germany that had a wonderful story of survival and triumph.

Her name was Pamela, and when she walked into the room, you could see that she wasn't walking quite normally. But you would never know that her story is one of her incredible attitude. After spending the week with her in the workshop and learning more about her, I was inspired to ask her to send me more details for this book. This is what I learned.

When she was fourteen, Pamela had a life threatening accident while riding her bicycle. A big lorry (truck) struck her and dragged her underneath it for about twelve meters (more than thirty-nine feet). As she was lying on the ground, screaming, her blood began pouring out of her body. Even as the paramedics arrived and transfused her, the new blood leaked out of her because of the extent of her injuries. Like me, she never lost consciousness, and, like me, she felt that the entire incident seemed surreal. It was as though she was watching it rather than living it. She was taken by helicopter to a hospital in Augsburg, Germany. The doctors were honest with her and told her that they were not capable of handling such severe injuries.

For this reason, she ended up being transferred to Munich, where they had a very good hospital and specialists that could save her life. She endured several operations during her ten week stay in the ICU. Although things looked bleak, she was holding on for dear life. Each night, she wondered if she would survive. She was given a one percent chance of survival, and even if she would survive, the doctors told her, she would spend the rest of her life in a wheelchair. They also told her parents that she would not be able to attend regular school and that she would never again live a normal life. She had several broken bones in her leg, damaged nerves, and wounds up and down her lower extremities. After one back operation, she was unable to move in any direction for eleven days as her body healed from the surgery. She was in so much pain that even morphine didn't help.

It took her several months just to sit up for a few minutes. After ten months, she was transferred to a new facility to do an extensive rehabilitation program. She was also instructed to learn to adjust to her new life in a wheelchair. The doctors and physiotherapists told her that the chance to stand up again was very slim, but Pam really wanted to walk again. She knew that she would have to work hard and endure great pain to have even the slightest chance to get back on her feet. After weeks of therapy, she tried to walk and fell down time after time. So she learned how to fall without hurting herself and got up every time she fell.

In the beginning, she told me, she also cried frequently and had many pity-parties for herself. As the rehabilitation went on, however, she focused on her goal of walking again and took a pragmatic approach—one step at a time both literally and figuratively. She practiced walking even when the physiotherapist was unavailable. She tried to stand in the swimming pool to build strength in her legs. Soon the tears that she wept out of self-pity turned into tears of pain because her intense recovery was so difficult. And, finally, those tears turned to joyful tears as she began to celebrate her own small victories.

When she left the rehabilitation facility, she went home with crutches rather than being rolled out in a wheelchair. She could see that her hard work was paying off and was more determined than ever to walk without help.

The doctors suggested that she go to a school for the handicapped, but she was determined to have some normalcy in her life and go back to her original school. When she returned to school, her friends encouraged her just as they had while she was in the hospital. The problem was that she had missed so much of the school year that her friends were ready to move to the tenth grade, but she didn't have enough hours to qualify for the next level. She was worried that she would lose her support system. She really wanted to be in the same grade as all of her friends.

One of the teachers at her school told her about a regulation that would allow someone to move up one grade level by testing as long as that student maintained grades that were better than the average for that grade. The message was clear: if her grades were higher than average, she would be allowed to join her friends in the tenth grade. For the next year, therefore, while her friends were busy going shopping, playing sports, and doing leisure activities, Pam concentrated on the two things that counted for her. She went to physiotherapy to learn to walk and she studied hard. What a burden to place on a fourteen-year-old!

Today, when you see Pam walk into a room, you don't see a victim. She doesn't ask for sympathy, nor does she act like someone who needs assistance. When she walks into the room, you can see that her gait is slightly off as she drags her leg a bit. But she always walks with confidence. Her eyes sparkle when she catches your gaze, and she always has a smile on her face. She doesn't focus on what she cannot do but relishes what she can do. She's willing to take on any new challenge. Pam arrived where she is today by never giving up and by always focusing on the small victories. She understands that she still has some limitations because of her injuries and she will never be like she was before the accident. For example, though she cannot walk long distances and it takes her longer to get anywhere, she doesn't focus on these limitations. Instead, she faces her new reality and just figures out how to avoid walking long distances. She also allows extra time so she can be on time.

Today, Pam has a very good job in the legal field. She does not have a normal life; she has an extraordinary life and works as a lawyer in an international aerospace company. She is also actively involved in JCI and is dedicated to creating positive change in the world. In addition to her success in her professional life, she is also focused on getting others to see past her handicap. Although she is independent and needs no one to survive, she has had the support of a strong family and developed many strong friendships over the years. She also found a wonderful man with a strong personality and a very good heart who accepts her as she is and loves her for her strength.

As I spoke with Pamela, I was enamored by her strong will. She told me that sometimes she meets people who see where she came from and where she is today and say to her, "Oh, you had such good luck to end up where you are." These people, she said, do not see her strong will and how hard she worked to where she is. She doesn't believe in good luck or bad luck. She feels that it was by keeping her faith and getting up every day to tackle the challenges in front of her that she was able to move forward in her new reality.

She also told me that people occasionally express pity and treat her differently. She doesn't want pity. Instead, she holds this philosophy. (1) If she can change it, then she fights for it. (2) If she cannot change it, she accepts it. When I asked her how she was able to survive her tragedy, which she has endured for practically her whole life, she told me that, first, she had to learn to be a fighter with a never-ending will to fight for success.

Second, she never gives up even if she fails again and again. Third, she never has an attitude of failure, a feeling that she cannot do something. She will try anything, and if it doesn't work, she looks for another way to do it. If that doesn't work, she keeps looking for a way. There is always a way.

The most important thing she told me was right in line with my own story. She does not waste time in negative emotions. She never indulges in self-pity. Instead, she concentrates on whatever she can do to make a situation more positive. She tries to set realistic goals and concentrates on reaching them. Then, as she meets a goal, she celebrates another victory.

When I heard her describe how she survived, I gave her a big hug and told her that I agree with everything she said. Our connection was instantaneous. I had finally found someone who wears a bigger medal on her chest than I do.

"But there is more," she said with a smile. I was already so enthralled with her story that I was celebrating her triumph without hearing the full message. She went on to talk about the key people in her life who encouraged her, including her father, who always gave her the will to keep moving forward and never give up. She surrounded herself with people who supported her decisions and were generally positive about what she was trying to do with her life and didn't waste time and energy on people who were not in line with her values. One of her biggest lessons was "Don't be what people want you to be. Be who you are and spend your life surrounded by people who love you because of who you are."

Hearing that, I asked her what values helped her through her tragedy. Of course, she listed being positive and encouraging others in the world, but she also talked about "being a candle in the night," having integrity and honesty, and treating others in a good way. Then she said something that really made me think.

"If you died tomorrow, what have you done for this world that changed it in a good way?"

When I didn't respond immediately, she reminded me that both of us received a second chance at life. Then she looked at me and said: "So what are you going to do with your second chance?"

At that point I knew that I had to write this book and share my story with people who might be going through their own tragedies. I also knew that I would have to include Pamela's story in this book. When she finally wrote her story down and sent it to me, I could tell that doing so was another step in her healing process.

She told me that her story is very personal and she usually doesn't share the details of her tragedy. But with her second chance, she felt that she wanted to put her story out there with the hope of encouraging people who are struggling with their own burdens.

"Never, never give up," she concluded. "Stand up, and you will make it through the rain to see the light shining through the clouds again."

Chapter Twenty-Two:

Moving Forward

Although it is always nice to hear someone tell me that they are inspired by the way I keep moving forward with life, I still struggle to understand the alternative. I truly believe that we all have the inner strength to survive a tragedy and move forward. This has been evident to me as I meet other survivors or when I read stories like those told in the previous chapters.

There are many people in this world who have endured worse tragedies than I have, yet they continue to move forward with their lives. They have stories that are rarely seen in the news media. But they are stories of hope and encouragement that should be shared with everyone. I found the following quote, which I believe sums up the will to move forward in these survivors:

> *Although it is tempting to resent disaster, there is not much use in doing so.... Whether we remain ash or become the phoenix is up to us.* —Deng Ming-Dao

Tragedies and obstacles in life can lead us to inner-growth. They give us opportunities to discover how much strength we have inside. When people tell me how strong I must be to have survived, I remind them that no one knows how much strength they have until they encounter great adversity. Most people have greater inner strength than they think. It is only through being resilient and moving forward against overwhelming odds that we can see our true strength.

It has also become clear to me that most people who have suffered loss or tragedy don't really want to be advised to move forward. It's too easy to tell someone to pick themselves up by the bootstraps and just get on with life. But when someone is suffering, he or she must be ready to move forward. They must want to move forward. Some people cannot move forward until they've had enough time to grieve, and others need to get past the shock that comes when you see the life you once knew vanish. Some people are ruled by their emotions. There's nothing wrong with being emotional, but that's not the approach I chose in my own recovery. I am quite pragmatic. I typically try to focus logically on moving forward, achieving the next goal, and celebrating each victory.

Of course, I grieved and cried and was very emotional. But I just kept looking for the next goal to get me through the misery. You might need to deal with a wide range of emotions, but I still encourage you to focus on those things you can control and place your trust in God that he will give you the strength you need.

After speaking with many other survivors, I have also learned that the timeframes for doing anything will vary widely from person to person. I discussed this earlier in regard to dating, but it generally applies to almost any area of your life. There is no authority that can tell you how long you should grieve or can give you an expected amount of time that you should be solemn out of respect for the departed. Nor, as I stated before, should you punish yourself out of some duty you think you owe to your deceased loved one. No book, no religious leader, no therapist, and no friend can tell you the timeframes that you have to follow in moving forward. Accept this as true, and you will have an easier time.

As I tried moving forward with my life, I encountered people who did not approve of my timeframes. Some of these people were friends of Lisa's. I understood why they might be upset when I started dating again. But there I was, thirty-seven years old, and I still wanted to have a family. I missed Lisa terribly, but I also knew that time was not on my side if I were to meet someone special, get married again, and start a family again. I had no intention of rushing anything. I wanted to find the right woman to share my life with. But I also didn't have the luxury of staying single for five years out of respect for my late wife. I decided right away that nobody would tell me how to live my life or make my life choices, especially if they hadn't walked in my shoes. When people sometimes made negative comments about what I was doing or how I was doing it, I gave my reasons and asked for their support. If they disapproved of my actions a second time, I told them that if I didn't have their support, I probably wouldn't be able to have them in my life. After a third criticism, I simply cut them out of my life and walked on. It sounds harsh and might not be the way you would operate, but so far, it has worked for me.

To survive this tragedy, get through the healing process, and move forward with my life, I knew that I had to look out for me first when it came to friends. I needed support, and if someone could not give it to me, I cut them from my life. Mostly, this happened when I started dating again. I asked my friends if they felt weird about that. My supportive friends told me if I was happy, then they were happy, too.

That being said, I do not judge the people with whom I disagree. As I sat in church one day, I listened carefully as the pastor talked about fully forgiving anyone you have perceived to have wronged you. In my heart, therefore, I forgive all the people who are no longer in my life for not understanding and not supporting me. At the same time, I ask for their forgiveness for seeming selfish and a little cold. There are no easy steps to take after a tragedy, but freely doling out forgiveness is one thing that is a must on all sides.

I used to be so concerned with wanting people to like me. This was especially true among my friends, coworkers, and JCI acquaintances. I always tried to be a good friend. I wanted them to think highly of me. When certain issues started to arise where people had bad reactions to what I was doing or even made impolite comments, I knew I would never be able to make everyone happy. Those days are long gone now. I know that my true friends will always be there for me.

One of my dearest friends, for example, had an issue

with my remarrying. She didn't approve of my marrying someone who was so different from Lisa. Her opinion hurt me tremendously because this was a person who was involved in my life and had been there through the good times, the bad times, and especially during my recovery. But after several discussions, we both realized that it was best to end our friendship. Emotions were high, and we both felt misunderstood. This is not to say my friend's reaction was wrong or that she had no justification for feeling as she did, but I could not have someone in my life who disapproved with my methodology of moving forward and could not be happy for me with my new life.

Of course, you never know what might happen in the future. For now, it's best for me to move forward with people who support my new life, whether they agree with it a hundred percent or not. I have forgiven the people who are no longer with me, and I hope that they forgive me as well.

My advice to others who experience tragedy is that you need to find your own formula for what works in putting the pieces back together. No single book or therapist or expert can give you all the answers. Once you are ready to move forward with your life and you have accepted that not everyone will approve of your timeframes, then you can begin to take certain actions that get the ball rolling. I don't have all the answers, but here are a few suggestions to begin the process:

Seek out those who care for and support you

As I stated above, for me, this was as simple as going back to St. Mary's Hospital and the Mt. Sinai Rehabilitation Center and seeing the joy on the faces of my doctors and nurses. I also found support among my closest friends and from around the world in JCI. There were people who came up to me after I gave a speech. There were my secretary and coworkers. And, of course, I always had my family. The key here is that you need to seek these people out and put yourself in activities that involve such people.

Share your thoughts

Not everyone will write a book or give a speech about what happened to them. But if you simply write down some of your thoughts, reactions, and experiences during the recovery process, doing this can have therapeutic healing effects. If you don't want to write the details, then have some meaningful conversations with people you trust and tell them how the situation has impacted you. Tell them about your new reality, your fears, and your challenges. Discuss how you plan to move forward and ask for their support.

Let people help you

I learned quickly that most people don't know how to react to people who have been touched by tragedy. They don't know what to say. They're not sure what they can do to help you. The reality is that they want to help you, and if you don't let them help you, then you're robbing them of the opportunity to show you how much they care. It makes them feel good to do something for you, so let them do something. When people walked into my hospital room for the first time and asked how they could help me, I always had an idea or a task to give to them. Sometimes I invented things for people to do for me just so they could feel like they were contributing to my recovery.

Limit your exposure to the news

If your tragedy involved a major accident or crime, it will probably be covered by all the media. Limit the amount of time you spend reading about your tragedy in newspapers. Be mindful of how much time you spend watching it on TV or how often you go to websites to read about it. Submerging yourself in the news of your tragedy can hobble your ability to move forward.

Realize that your reactions are normal

After a tragedy, we tend to fear that our feelings and reactions are inappropriate or irrational. It is important to realize that each person's reaction to tragedy is his or her normal response to a very abnormal experience. Our feelings and reactions may be completely different from other peoples', but how we feel is our normal—and often unique—way of coping with the loss.

Gain perspective--speak with a trusted person

A fresh pair of eyes can be useful in helping you deal with your emotions. Seek a wider perspective by speaking with a therapist, pastor, priest, mentor, or someone else who has been through a similar experience. Friends and family can be great supporters, but sometimes you need a more objective point of view that is not so close to the situation.

Consider joining a support group

These days, it seems that there's a support group to help us through almost any kind of situation. Consider finding a support group of people who are going through the same kind of experience as yours, or one similar to it. Make sure that the group is right for you. After my incident, I checked out a support group for "young" widows and widowers. As it turns out, most of the people in this group were between forty-five and fifty-five, more than ten years older than I was. They had very different needs than I did. Although the people were wonderful and the idea was good, this group was not a good fit for me, so I didn't try to force it to be the right one. I kept looking.

Stay financially sound

When you have suffered great injury or when you have lost a spouse, the financial burden can be tremendous. Just the sheer amount of paperwork can be overwhelming. Keeping up can feel like a full-time job. I am a lawyer with an accounting background, and I still had difficulty dealing with the insurance, medical bills, disability policies, probate issues, and tax ramifications of my tragedy. I recommend that you find a trusted friend that can help you find an attorney, financial advisor, accountant or whatever other professional you need to guide you through the process. If you don't have the money to hire someone, then go to a legal aid clinic or at the very least, ask friends or relatives who have good heads on their shoulders to help you through the paperwork.

Use visualization techniques

Dr. Schram gave me an invaluable tool for dealing with intense situations. It helped me get through that first day back in my house and also many other times when I knew my emotions would be high. I also used it for the killer's plea conference. Visualization can be useful before seeing friends for the first time, when thinking about difficult questions you may be asked by strangers, when you have to deal with the press, or when you start thinking about the limitations of your new reality. Basically, you can use your visualization exercise for any situation that might put emotional or mental stress on you.

See the big picture

You will likely live a long, fruitful life. When tragedy strikes, it can have long-lasting effects, but it's only a part of the whole of your life. You cannot let it consume you to the point that it becomes your identity. See your recovery as an opportunity to overcome obstacles and make you a more valuable person. Realize that you still have many years to create memories, help others, and lead a good life.

Stay healthy

Some people tend to shut down after tragedy strikes. Understandably, they're in shock and are probably grieving. However, you must make sure that you get outside, get some exercise, sleep enough hours, see your friends, and eat well. Taking care of your physical state has a tremendous effect on your psychological well-being.

Reminisce about past victories and successes

While I was in the hospital, in order to cheer myself up and kill some time, I daydreamed about earlier times in my life when I had experienced joy. What I thought about were past victories or successes, like trials and sporting events I won and speeches in which I was "on." Other things I remembered were moments I had shared with my mother or brothers or friends. By revisiting these memories, I often brought myself back into good spirits. They gave me renewed motivation to create new successes in my life and to seek out new opportunities of joy.

Count your blessings and realize it could always be worse

No matter what you're going through in your life, there is probably someone out there who has it worse. For me, being in a coma was bad, but losing my legs would have been worse. Losing your job is bad, but losing a spouse is worse. Alfredo Bless helped me learn this lesson the day he rolled into my hospital room.

Instead of focusing on how bad your situation is, make a list of your blessings. Maybe you have a healthy child, full eyesight, a roof over your head. List everything from the big stuff to the tiniest, most overlooked blessings in your life, like breathing or waking up each morning. Thinking of the good things will help you refocus your energy and put you in the right state of mind.

Stop worrying about the future

Take it one step at a time. Deal with your real present issues rather than worrying about what might possibly happen in the future. It's easy to overwhelm yourself with possibilities and outcomes that you can't see, and I'm sure you can imagine many crazy scenarios or envision future obstacles that cannot be conquered. Stop! Don't do it anymore. Take things one day at a time, keep moving forward, and try to embrace your reality without fearing the unknown.

Chapter Twenty-Three:

Perfectly Blessed

If you were to view my life in a vacuum on November 26, 2009, it looked like I was truly blessed in every way. Fast forward to February 24, 2012. If you view my life in a vacuum, things are perfect and I feel truly blessed in every way. This is one hundred percent true. In the two years after I was shot, things happened very quickly as I concentrated on moving forward with my life and embracing my new reality. During those two years, every piece of my life was miraculously put back together.

Not everyone will move forward at such a fast pace, but for me, it felt natural, so I embraced it. God has truly blessed me tenfold with a new life full of joy, hope and peace.

What has made my life truly perfect is the fact that I fell in love with a gorgeous young woman named Jennifer, who has now become my partner in life. I knew that God had sent her to me because of the circumstances of our meeting. She had an assistant who was a cousin of my secretary. After the cousins set us up on a date, we realized that we had everything in common. The chemistry was so strong between us that I knew from the beginning that she was the woman for me. She is my dream girl. I knew instantly that this was the woman with whom I wanted to build a family, and I feel blessed that God sent her to me.

Our background and upbringings were nearly identical. We both have good, Christian, Midwestern parents and backgrounds. I grew up in Illinois. She was born in Indiana and grew up in Minnesota and Kentucky. We share the same sense of humor and we have laughed almost every day since the day we met. She was supportive of me from day one.

Physically, I feel as if I have returned to my old body in almost every way. Granted, I am missing a kidney and have some huge scars on my torso, but if you saw a picture of me before the shooting and a picture of me today (in clothes, of course), I look nearly the same. I lost fifty-five pounds while I was in the coma, but my muscles have now returned to my body. I look healthy and, more importantly, I feel healthy.

One interesting aspect of my body's rebirth was Jennifer's reaction when I first began dating her. At the time, I was able to walk fairly well, but I was still learning to run again, and I certainly couldn't use weights because my wrists weren't working yet. I had balance problems and I wasn't even able to get off the floor easily without assistance.

As we spent more time together, she asked me at one point if I wanted to go running outside for exercise with her. I had tried to run a few times, but it hadn't gone well. The first time I tried to jog, I ran with the spastic motion we see in little kids running outside for recess. So I was just starting to get the hang of running again when Jennifer asked me to go outside and try it with her. I agreed and prayed to God for strength (and to keep me from looking like a spazz).

As we began to run, I lasted about a hundred yards, but then I told her to hold up. I couldn't get enough oxygen in my lungs as my chest started heaving up and down. We walked a bit, then tried running again. We made it for another hundred yards before I had to stop, again doubled over in exhaustion. This happened seven or eight times more as we jogged around a lake. It was disheartening for me because I used to be an athlete, but now I couldn't even run a hundred yards.

As I started to run more regularly, my legs got bigger and bigger. Even without using weights, my upper body also began to grow as a result of picking up boxes and living my normal life. I saw Jennifer every few days, and one day she hugged me and said, "It seems like you're growing bigger every time I see you."

That was true. I was. Muscle memory is amazing and my body was literally growing every single day. I could see my arms and chest getting bigger. Those size medium shirts I bought after leaving the hospital were now fitting me so snugly that I had to give them away.

In fact, I was often in pain for many months after I left the hospital because my muscles were constantly growing. But I was determined to get better, so we began to exercise more and more. My lung capacity got better, my muscles got stronger, and within a few months, I was able to run one mile, then two miles, then three miles. My body was getting back into shape. I thanked God for giving me the strength to run and putting Jennifer in my life to support and encourage me. I was always sore and my muscles would give out sometimes, but I never gave up.

By December, 2010 (about ten months after I woke up), my brother Brian and I stood at the starting line for the Muddy Buddy race in Miami. This was the race he'd told me he'd signed us up for when I still couldn't move. This was the race I had daydreamed about in the hospital and afterward. And now here we were among 2,000 competitors for a six-mile running and biking team race. I was excited. I didn't do quite as well as I had done the year before, of course. I couldn't run the entire distance and had to walk a bit, but I crossed the finish line with Brian and we celebrated a huge victory. We didn't win the race, but I won something bigger.

I can now physically do everything I could do before, all the athletics. Jennifer and I routinely run three miles around the lake several times a week. When I go to the gym, I don't lift heavy weights anymore, but I have realized that I could if I wanted to. The muscles have come back. I go trail bike riding with Brian, I run ten to twelve miles a week, and I just generally feel like I can do things again. In December, 2011, we competed in the Muddy Buddy race for the third time and did much better. You know what? My new "normal" is pretty darn good.

My wrists also woke up. My left wrist woke up about eight months after I did, but my right wrist took a little over a year to fully wake up. There are no braces on my hands anymore. I can play golf, basketball, and football, and I can even hit a one-handed backhand in tennis. There was no guarantee that my wrists would wake up, and I had adapted many of my activities to deal with my wrists working at half strength. But I believe God rewarded me because I never became upset with my situation. I just kept on in my new reality and embraced everything that came my way.

As I wrote above, just over eight months after I woke up from the coma, I traveled to Osaka, Japan, to speak at the JCI World Congress. As many times as I had envisioned the moment, nothing could compare to the actual feeling of walking on stage. The excitement in the room that day was palpable. I can still remember the announcer saying, "Welcome, ladies and gentlemen, to the JCI Morning Show. Please put your hands together for our speaker this morning. From Miami Florida, Patrick Knight."

The standing ovation was amazing, but the impact that the audience had on me went deeper than that. As I spoke, I could see people wiping tears from their eyes as they reacted to my description of the shooting itself. I also watched them sit upright, smile, and nod as I talked about the triumph of overcoming the tragedy. I could see and feel that these people wanted to share in the hope that my story brings to people who can start to realize that they, too, can move forward from their problems. It was an eye-opening epiphany, and I was very grateful for the opportunity.

When I think back to that moment, I realize that this was what Pamela was talking about when she asked me what I would do with my second chance. It was the beginning of what I was going to do with my second chance. Speeches I gave in Detroit and Osaka let me see that my message resonates with people. I want to help those who are struggling to overcome tragedy. But God's plan for me is much greater than one or two speeches. I now have a goal to reach as many people as possible and give them hope for their new reality.

As promised, my boss held my job for me. I went back to work three weeks after I left the rehabilitation facility and conducted my first trial two months later. I won that trial. Since that time, I have had many trials and have returned to a full caseload. When I was lying in the hospital bed, it seemed totally unrealistic to think I would be able to be a trial lawyer again, but I feel as comfortable as ever in the courtroom.

My life as a speaker and trainer has also returned in a spectacular way. First, I now have a very compelling story to share with the world. I used to give seminars only on leadership, business, and communications. Now I spend half my time as a speaker sharing my story and talking about my heavenly strength coach.

In 2011, I was named the JCI Training Chairperson for the entire world. I led an international team of training commissioners from Belgium, Nigeria, Suriname, and India as we organized seminars around the world and certified up-and-coming international trainers. We even developed two training manuals to teach advanced training techniques to professional speakers and trainers.

With all of these blessings, however, I still had to deal with the killer and his trial. Although I had mostly put the tragedy behind me, the media was constantly following the story of the shooting and speculating as to whether or not the killer would be brought to justice. Originally, the prosecutors sought the death penalty. But the killer countered with a defense of insanity. In mid-2011, his attorneys approached the prosecutors and asked for a plea deal. If the prosecutors would take the death penalty off of the table, the killer would plead guilty to the murders, drop the insanity defense, and accept seven consecutive life sentences. The prosecutors brought the offer to me and explained all the possible angles and options.

I was tired of all the media attention to the shooting and the killer's trial. I didn't want to have to go through a trial myself and deal with the circus-like atmosphere that the media would bring to it. Moreover, I was concerned that if the defense was able to convince a jury of insanity, the killer could be back on the street within a few years after a stint at a mental health hospital.

That's why I agreed with the prosecutors to accept the plea deal and the seven consecutive life sentences. It assured me that the killer would never walk the streets again. He would be sent to a maximum security prison and have to live with the worst criminals, including other murderers. His seven consecutive life sentences without the possibility of parole meant that I would never have to worry about seeing the killer again. I would never have to even think about him.

With the killer's plea conference behind me, I was able to focus on my new life and the blessings God has put in it. Jennifer and I took a five-day trip to Rome in

January, 2011, a romantic and magical trip. On the final night, we went out to a nice dinner and then walked through the streets of Rome. It was nearly 3 a.m. when we reached the Trevi Fountain. We had it all to ourselves. After tossing a coin in, I got down on one knee and proposed to her. Jennifer and I were married in the spring of 2011.

Now I am truly living the life that God wants for me. He has blessed me with the opportunity to have another family and has given me a wife who is perfect for me in every way. One would think that this would have been a difficult situation given my incident, my recovery, and the way many people would view me post-shooting. But Jennifer has supported me at every step. We did not have to force anything because it just seemed so natural, so right.

When I wake up in the morning, the bad things are all gone. I used to wake up in pain, depressed, and defeated. It used to end with me staring into my cereal as the tears dripped off my nose and into the milk. Today, I look over and see my lovely wife, who makes my life complete. I lean over and give her a kiss. I reach down and pet my dogs, who are nuzzled up against my legs.

I move my arms and realize that my wrists work perfectly. I can sit up without getting dizzy, and it only takes me one try. I smile as I see the sun shining through the window. When I get out of bed and put my feet on the floor, it's not a struggle. In fact, I don't even think about it. I walk without a problem to the bathroom, and when I look at the huge scars on my torso, I don't see defeat. I see victory.

With these new blessings, Jennifer and I live the life we both always wanted. Every day when I come home, I just look around at all my blessings. Our house sits on a big lake, and I love looking out into the water, which is calm and peaceful. I enjoy playing and running around the yard with our two little dogs. Yes, this is the life I have always wanted.

Just because I feel blessed, however, does not mean that every piece of news is good. Even though I feel and act healthy, I have to constantly be monitored for kidney and blood pressure issues. Two years after I woke up, I had blood work done to assess the level of function in my remaining kidney. When I went for the next doctor visit, he gave me some grim news. He told me that I have stage three chronic kidney disease in the one kidney I have left. At stage four, they begin monitoring you very closely to see if you need a transplant. Stage five is complete kidney failure. The doctor told me that I have the kidney function of an eighty-five-year-old man.

This was horrible news. I left the doctor's office, got into my car, and began to cry. Everything seemed so perfect, and now this news had caught me off guard. After half an hour of crying and driving, I remembered the strategy I had used for getting through all those pity-parties. I took a deep breath, counted my blessings, and realized that I had my work cut out for me.

From that moment forward, I started eating a very healthy, kidney-friendly diet. I focused on keeping in great shape through exercise, and I am extra-careful to make sure that I take my blood pressure medication. My kidney is operating at a just-below-normal function right now, but there is no reason that I can't keep it at that level for the rest of my life.

I was so proud of myself for controlling that new pity-party and immediately getting off the stool to get back into the ring. But when you have a divine strength coach like mine, it gives you the confidence to reach for any goal. Life isn't always easy or fair, but I certainly feel blessed to be alive.

Most recently, God has blessed me again. Jennifer and I now have a son named Lucas. Who would have believed that only two and a half years after the worst tragedy in my life, God would fill my life with this many blessings? I couldn't wait to have children to fill the house with laughter and energy, and now God has helped me begin that process. My life is perfect, and I thank God every day for that. These days, my prayers for strength are outnumbered by my prayers of thanks.

I believe God gave me this new life—this perfect life—because my faith never wavered, because I trusted my strength coach, because I never gave up, and because I made the choice to get out of bed each day. I am not special, nor do I take all the credit for moving forward all by myself from this tragedy. God has a plan for each and every one of us. He will be there to guide us through the process of moving forward. If you have faith and seek his strength, God will give you the life you seek. It is up to you to seek it.

Chapter Twenty-Four:
Everything Will Be Okay in the End

*In the end, everything will be okay. If it's not okay,
it's not the end.* —Unknown

A court reporter friend of mine gave me this quote
while we were waiting for a jury to come back with a
verdict in one of my trials. I think it sums up what I
have written in this book pretty well. It's so simple. If
you keep moving forward, counting your blessings and
avoiding pity-parties, things will eventually be okay.
There is no timeframe for your recovery, so if it's not
okay yet, then you're not at the end.

The reality is that you might never truly be "at the
end" of your recovery. Life is a journey with many twists
and turns. You will change many times during the course
of your life journey, but you must always remain true
to your core values and principles. Your number-one
priority should be your faith in God, followed by your
commitment to your family and to yourself. After going

through adversity, you still have amazing qualities as a person, and now you have an incredible life experience that validates your sense of worth.

For some people, this quote may seem to imply something it really doesn't say. Some might think it's suggesting that there's no need to try because you can just wait it out and things will be okay. I suggest they need to go back and read Chapter 15 about getting off the stool. I believe the point is that you need to keep trying to move forward and keep putting your trust in God.

I started writing this book within four months of leaving the hospital. I knew it would be therapeutic for me, but I also wanted to capture the raw emotion of things as they were happening I felt that it was important for readers to share my experiences as they were occurring, so that it didn't seem like a fluff-piece that was easy to write once my life got back on track. I still don't know the meaning of my survival, but you can already see what I'm doing with my second chance.

If you've lived through a tragedy, you can think of your recovery the same way you think about living your life in general. We are always trying to search for the meaning of life. Most likely, you will now also search for the meaning of your tragedy and your recovery. It's a never-ending journey that should be embraced rather than feared.

Many people go through the motions of life and never have the opportunity to experience true sadness or true joy. If you've been faced with tremendous catastrophe, you've proved that you can survive. Surely now you will seek out those moments of joy and elation that make life worth living, but you will never forget the tragedy that exists in this world.

If there is one thing that you take from this book, I hope that you realize that God has given you the strength to get through your issues. It's up to you, however, to find the attitude to match this gift of strength. You can find inspiration all around you. There are support and love all around you that you need to embrace. You have the strength to move forward, but it's up to you – and only you - to take a step. Get off your stool and get back into the fight.

CPSIA information can be obtained at www.ICGtesting.com
Printed in the USA
BVOW082355150812

297843BV00001B/39/P

9 780985 690502